Energizing Love

Achieving Abundant Life using the Source of All Energy, UILE[1]

Energizing Love

Achieving Abundant Life using the Source of All Energy, UILE[1]

Phil 'Philosofree' Cheney

CHRISTIAN ALTERNATIVE

Winchester, UK
Washington, USA

First published by Christian Alternative Books, 2015
Christian Alternative Books is an imprint of John Hunt Publishing Ltd.,
Laurel House, Station Approach,
Alresford, Hants, SO24 9JH, UK
office1@jhpbooks.net
www.johnhuntpublishing.com
www.christian-alternative.com

For distributor details and how to order please visit the 'Ordering' section on our website.

ISBN: 978 1 78535 061 0
Library of Congress Control Number: 2015932359

A CIP catalogue record for this book is available from the British Library.

Design: Stuart Davies

Printed and bound in the USA by Edwards Brothers Malloy

CONTENTS

Invitation

I am an Executive Life Coach, and my aim is to draw out the potential you have within you. I do this without judgment, or prejudice.

There may be new concepts in here that challenge how you taste the world.

You cannot eat unless you put food in your mouth and swallow, it is your choice. Nothing I say is intended to control what you believe.

You are being invited to try a smorgasbord of tastes that may be different to your taste buds. However the ingredients are from the same garden you love, I just hope the recipe may be new.

Consumption of the dishes presented is optional; my intention is that you find it appealing to your particular palate.

Prologue

Song of joy.

Light lances my being, releasing a song of joy.
I cannot understand.
It is the song of those who fly above echoes,
The song of soul sifted through skin.

Drink from the bowl of heaven's grace.
Let your hair be wet with the generous rain of truth
Our breath is a golden knowing, like the first sight of dawn.
Our awaked-ness is a bright star calling the rays of the rising sun.

Lie in the dark earth and be embraced by warm light.
Let your heart leap like a puppy,
And your thoughts bind to the will of the one creator of all.
Like emerald water in the sand, let the thoughts of the creator enter your being.

Based on Egyptian writings circa 2000 BC.

Once I stood on a cliff overlooking the Southern Ocean, watching seagulls gliding on the updraft, and I experienced a sense of lightness that covered me, lifted me, like I was one of those seagulls. Standing on that cliff edge I felt like I was leaning out into the updraft of faith, and had an understanding of what it was like going past the edge, flying like Peter Pan, without fear. For a while I imagined I could float past the strikingly blue sky out beyond the moon, the stars, even the galaxies, while my body stayed firmly on the ground.

I would like to have a name for that part of me that entered that blissful state, because I would like to have stayed there.

Some have called this essence 'soul', others the 'golden world', some 'nirvana', but I am disappointed with these words, because they don't fully describe what I was experiencing. I just knew I was limitless, and connected with love.

There are elements of our being that we can name without too much difficulty. "Body", "Thought", "Experience" and "Senses" are examples that appear at first glance to be controllable. However, "Emotions", and "Dreams", though closely connected, appear outside conscious control as they emerge from within. Then consider the autonomous nervous system, breathing, and the heart function that operate while we are asleep or awake, we cannot claim conscious control for these either. In fact, reality is an awakening that I cannot control anything but my own conscious thought patterns, and then at times I have trouble with these too!

Have you had thought streams at times where you wanted to stop thinking of that extra cookie, or the offense you took at some random comment, or an image from a horror movie that repeats like garlic breath for which you have no freshening mouth wash? I have. Thinking assumes individuality, that we are separate and in control. But we know there are unconscious voices from within that we struggle with, that go against our conscious desires.

From where did we inherit the thinking that our life is individual? Let me introduce two new terms, Negative-Ego[2] and UILE[1]. Negative-Ego is a parasite that has no mass, yet it is a seed that is in every human, and infiltrates our thought patterns just like those unwanted and persistent thought patterns above.

Negative-Ego is a sort of cancer that grows on the concept that any human is individual, and it grows fast when it is fed the notion that the human is a disconnected and bad, sinful, being.

Negative-Ego is the internal source of judgment and blame, and the concepts of 'control', 'take' and 'greed'. It is also the only thing that we need control over, once we recognize its existence. But most importantly, it is the ONLY obstacle stopping our beings from entering that blissful space of peace and joy that I first described.

UILE is an old Irish word, pronounced like '**willeh**', meaning "*All, whole, wholly, all things* or *entirely*". It is derived from the proto-Celtic 'Olyo'[3]. In this book I will later define and use UILE[1] in a specific way. As it is a new word in your vocabulary, it comes with no baggage, so you can elect to interpret it as it seems to work for you.

I believe we limit ourselves because we have been taught to do so. This book is intended to help remedy the false perception that life is a pain in the ass. That is a common belief of those who don't know an alternative. If you currently feel trapped, please open yourself to a new possibility. If you desire to be anyone else other than who you are, please ask yourself why. Your life is as valuable as any other. Don't diminish the source of love within yourself.

Would you like to live in bliss and a sense of abundance, even if others act in ways intended to put you down? The solution is inside you. It is discovered by understanding that you are part of the wonder of Universal Energy, and this book can help you to be all you truly are, and enter abundance *now*. It will also outline where you belong and why.

When I started writing, I didn't set out to do anything other than document and share why my heart is so open, and full of joy, less than 10 years after the impact of losing my dear only son. During the process of writing I was inspired by wisdom from many varied and rich sources, from science, from psychology, from all forms of art, spirituality, philosophy, quantum physics, biology, mathematics, humor and from my friends.

After consideration of why I now feel so connected and at peace, I believe it is because of Love. A love that is reflected from my darling partner Manu, but also in dance, music and every life I encounter. I have found that life is *meant* to be abundant within. You gain your bliss by returning to your true self.

It may sound easy but it means giving up a lot of habitual thinking.

That is why I wrote this book. Because there is so much unnecessary waste of life, not just in war but in systems of thinking that diminish life. I want to show that life is meant to be abundance, bliss, and joy, even when there is severe loss and confusion.

We are sailing this unique life not towards a set destination, but on a vacation where we are free to change to match with our heart's desire or with the important messages of our passengers or the weather. We can stop when we wish. We can stay as long as we need. But we should not sail again till the spirit winds are blowing in a direction away from our current port, even if that port is a prison of learning.

Therefore, I disagree with ordering people what to believe. It doesn't make sense. Should I come across as instructional, please ignore any such interpretation and accept that these are my views placed on the sushi train of options available. I merely ask you to consider the passing parade and choose those dishes that sit comfortably with who you truly are.

I am in love with life, and I hope that my enthusiasm is contagious! (Sort of like how yawning or smiling can be contagious.)

I welcome you to a philosophy of abundant life!

Section One – Energy, UILE, Space

Chapter 1

The Nature of Energy

Quantum physicists have learned that there is no physical substance inside atoms; the sub-units that comprise atoms are made out of extremely powerful invisible energy vertices
Professor Bruce Lipton

You are pure energy! Seriously.

Everything, all matter, is made up of energy.

(Bear with me if you happen to feel drained and out of energy right now.)

Energy is involved in every beat of your heart, every breath you take. Energy exists in many forms. Energy can have the form of sound (music), electric, chemical, magnetic, potential, and gravitational force, all of which are able to transfer between one another. For example, potential energy can become kinetic energy like when a suspended rock falls. Chemical energy can become heat energy when a chemical reaction occurs. Atomic energy can become light and heat in nuclear fission.

A really powerful example of energy transformation is a lightning strike, where up to 500 mega joules of electric potential energy is converted into the same amount of energy in other forms, most notably light energy, sound energy and thermal energy in a single flash of lightning! Oh, by the way, energy cannot be destroyed, only converted into other forms of energy, or mass.[4]

Now imagine all the energy in the sun. A handful of the sun brought close to earth would fry everything. Imagine all the suns in our galaxy, the Milky Way; millions of them. Now add all the stars of all the galaxies that exist. You get my drift? This is a lot of energy.[5]

All of this amazing group of energies could be called the Universal set of Energy. Universal Energy is my term for the summation of all energies of all forms. Universal Energy is therefore a very immense concept. It may seem too hard, even inconceivable; all the energy from all the suns in all the vast and innumerable galaxies, plus more. OK come back to earth now. I want to show you that all this energy is not only a single *relevant* whole, but you are a *relative*.

While humankind relies on energy sources, energy is something humans can only understand through observation or experience within the finite, and scientists are still working hard to get a grasp on the way energy exhibits itself. There is mystery in energy. Everything that you experience involves this mysterious force.

You experience energy in many ways such as:

- Heat on your skin.
- Sound in your ears.
- Gravity pulling down on your body!

The brain can only function if it is activated by electrical energy because the brain processes like a computer, in that both have complex circuitry that utilizes an electric current. In fact the brain consumes 20% of the energy of the body, and it is one of the organs that signify death, when electric pulses are no longer evident. In other words, without energy, your body does not have life.

The force of attraction is not just pulling at your body, in different ways it also affects how you think, what passions you have, and how you see yourself. Energy is an integral part of everything you truly are and desire.

Have I lost you in science? Maybe this will help. When I was a kid I used to enjoy licking the empty cans of condensed milk that my mum sometimes used. The milk was very thick because a lot of milk was boiled down to a thick paste. Well you are a tin of condensed energy! OK that's not true, there is no tin container. But you are made up of matter, and matter is a sort of condensed energy.

Energy can be converted into matter.[6] At this time humans have only been able to create sub-atomic matter from energy.[7] Creating matter, something that appears solid mass, from this strange concept we call energy has been achieved. The energy of a gram of matter is a lot! A gram of matter converted into heat (as happens in an atomic bomb explosion) is sufficient to destroy a city, and it conversely takes the same amount of energy to create a gram of matter. To illustrate, a few grams of matter converted to energy in a nuclear power station is sufficient to power a city like New York for a month. A single uranium fuel pellet the size of a fingertip contains as much energy as 17,000 cubic feet of natural gas, and that pellet only marginally decreases in mass during its fission. Imagine how much energy it would take to create a human body? That energy is within you. You are indeed a container of condensed energy!

You may find this concept hard to comprehend but it is one of many Quantum Physics laws and theories that have been postulated during my lifetime. Does it surprise you that;

- Time only exists when matter exists.[8]
- Energy in the form of light, and electric and magnetic fields all travel through space. How?[9]
- Electrons can behave in a plasma as if they are part of an interconnected whole (Plasmons) which is organized and life-like.
- Empty space is not empty.[10] It is in fact full of energy.

These examples are all based on observable scientific evidence.

The 'Big Bang' is the prevailing scientific theory that explains the early development of the Universe. The Big Bang theory states that all matter originated from a single point of energy which exploded to fill the infinite depths of space with matter. This is the only current explanation as to why the galaxies all appear to be moving away from a single point.[11] The scientific conclusion is that everything originates from energy.

"Everything in this Universe is made out of immaterial energy, and everything radiates energy."[12]

As everything is made up of energy, including the chair you are sitting on, the dog at your feet, and the light that allows you to read this, I invite you to accept that your body is also made up of energy.

Quantum Theory is the study of energy, which we now understand to exist in discrete units which behave like particles (sub-atoms if you will). At some level, particles and energy appear to interchange. Particles emit energy, and have a connection through that, a form of communication which is not fully understood. All we know is that every particle knows what every other particle it has ever interacted with is doing, via radiant energy. This is not some weirdo thought I have dreamt up, this is the best understanding of the physical basis of the scientific world we live in. A key philosophy in this new awareness of Quantum Physics is that energy forms the basis for everything, and is able to communicate!

Unconvinced? That is ok. It is healthy to consider the concepts of Quantum Physics and Universal Energy with a high degree of mystery, as it is indeed mind boggling. And it gets even more interesting!

Here is another interesting scientific observation. Because of the crossover between mass and energy, the current best scientific way to describe the smallest sub-atomic particles is as a wave form. (In simplified form, the tiniest bits of matter are constructed of energy.)

Because I love music, I have this happy picture in my mind of the entire universe being made up of little waves of music energy. Most people can relate to this image, because music is about patterns, harmony and good vibes. There is another aspect to this though. If everything we observe is actually energy, it deserves more of our attention, like, does energy have intelligence, or is the communication of energy what we understand as intelligence? Another way of asking this is; is there composition of the music at the base of all existence, or are we a score in a universal symphony?

Let's consider if there is any scientific support for the intentionality of life. I recently was introduced to the fascinating terms *teleology* and *teleonomy*[13]. Teleology says that there is intention in nature, in other words that nature is a planned or purposeful event. That can be external design (some intelligence is leading this) or internal (the organism works out its own goal – e.g. a seed has intent to become a tree). Teleology was first recorded with Aristotle in ancient Greece, and is still relevant, because the complexity of life shows astounding direction and purpose.

A classic example of external design is the migration of birds. For a bird species to have a migratory capability to fly to a particular location, and then to get back again to the same location where it was born on the other side of the world, only makes sense to me in a context of their knowing of something better, a yearning for change, a source energy of intelligence. How do we explain that Acacia trees in Africa have the intention to warn other Acacia trees of incoming threat?[14] Is that not targeted societal intent within nature?

It should not surprise you that humans are even more capable of societal transmission than birds or trees. Teressa Fenison explains that *"Morphogenic or Morphogenetic fields are fields of energy containing a certain frequency or resonance, created by all living species that are both visible and invisible on planet Earth. All living species, human beings, animals and plants have a consciousness and therefore an emotional field."*

The Princeton Engineering Anomalies Research (PEAR)

program was established at Princeton University in 1979 by Robert G. Jahn, an aerospace engineer who was then Dean of the School of Engineering and Applied Science. They concluded that remote perception via connected thought of another human (target) is a capacity of human consciousness, and is also largely independent of the distance between the percipient and the target, and similarly independent of the time between the specification of the target and the perception effort. The results yielded a probability against chance of approximately three parts in ten billion.

Can human thought energy also be demonstrated to have a causal effect on matter? There is evidence to suggest so. There have been some scientific experiments on the effect of thought, which is a form of electrical impulse energy, on matter.[15] *(This book is not predicated on this research incidentally, it just offers a new insight to consider how intentional energy could have effect on matter.)*

However, you don't need a scientific program to prove what you observe in your own life, that some awareness of, and influence over others, happens by your presence or thought alone. Some call this meditation or prayer; others call it mindfulness or focusing.

There are ancient traditions of energy as a life force in many civilizations. Life-force energy is the concept of energy that flows through all living things. It is well known and accepted in the East, known as Ki in Japan, chi (Qi) in China, Prana in India and many other names in other cultures.

So, let's summarize what we just learned about energy thus far:

- It exists,
- We can see its effects,
- We can measure it,
- It can be created from matter in a nuclear reactor, and
- Conversely energy can create matter!

- It also has the ability to influence or communicate with matter and life forms, and
- At the primal level, matter is a form of energy.

Consider now if energy was also supremely creative and *intentional,* in other words that it could conceive the creation of being from its own non-being!

Humans are just beginning to investigate the world in a different way. We already know that energy is within us, and can be used to create, matter. We know that energy binds the atomic matter of earth and the universe, and therefore is the building block for the more complex matter of living things. In his 1925 book,*Science and the Modern World,* Alfred North Whitehead[16] concluded that everything changes over time, and to think of anything as having an "*enduring essence*" misses that fact that "*all things flow. All things have some measure of freedom or creativity.*" This leads to the conclusion that intentional creation will include freedom and creativity.

Panpsychism is the view that mind or soul (Greek: psychē means "life, spirit, consciousness") is a universal feature of all things living and inert, and that all matter has consciousness. The philosopher Thomas Nagel argues that a shift to panpsychism is now necessary to understand the cosmos[17]. Panpsychism is one of the oldest philosophical theories, and it is the basis of most indigenous people's belief in the presence of a united spirit or psyche within everything, from a rock, to a plant to every animal. It is also closely related to Animism (Latin: animus means "soul, life") which is the belief that all entities, including animals, plants, and inanimate objects or phenomena, possess a spiritual essence. The difference between panpsychism and animism is in the understanding of there being one mind in all, or many spirits or minds.

Not surprisingly, panpsychism has significantly influenced structured major religions too, for example in Christianity via

Plato, and in Mahayana Buddhism. Indeed, M Scott Peck, psychologist and the author of the best-selling book, *The Road Less Travelled* states that "*mysticism is essentially a belief that reality is oneness*" and that "*Our common perception of the universe as containing multitudes of discrete objects – stars, trees, birds, ourselves – all separated from one another by boundaries is a misperception, an illusion.*"[18]

But does the universe have the elements of panpsychic intelligence? Many Quantum physicists now acknowledge that reality is based on

- experience,
- the consciousness of each observer,
- that there is a fourth dimension which is time related, and that
- matter as we know it is constructed from "*quantized fields made up of both wave-like and particle-like characters*".[19]

We may now conclude that all the elements of a quantum computer, time-based processing, infinite data storage via quantum information[20], and of course energy flow, all are ubiquitously present across the universe.

If we can accept a premise that a super-computer, which relies on energy, can have a form of intelligence[21], then surely this vast universe of energy and quantum information could too. Universal Energy *could* be intentionally focused, in other words there is reason to believe that Universal Energy empowers a united intelligence behind all existence. We cannot prove this empirically, but our heart can lead the way.

"It is true that we look as if we are physical, but it is an illusion, a trick of the light – we are all energy."[22]

The breath of life itself, the mystery of life, its complexities and wonder, could be one and the same with the breath of Universal Energy. Mystery is at the heart of scientific knowledge, so don't be afraid of it, embrace it. Mystery is recognizing that there are some things that we just don't know, but that life is greater for believing in.

Hence I have concluded that all we observe and experience is created by Universal Energy, an instantiation which I will refer to as UILE, pronounced like '*willeh*', which is an ancient Celtic word meaning 'whole' or 'all'. Serendipitously, it also is an acronym standing for **U**niversal **I**ntentional **L**ove **E**nergy, which is all wholeness or holiness empowering a united ethical intent. This 'Intentional Love' includes, but is a much larger concept than, human love, as it is truly All, the Universal Spirit of mankind, or the Source, so bear with me until I define UILE further in the next chapter.

I believe that Intentional Love, then, is one of the defining attributes of **U**niversal **I**ntentional **L**ove **E**nergy, to which all creation, all other energies, belong, and I believe that UILE has intentional purpose for all life, including yours.

The notion that Intentional Love is energy is a basic premise on which I will be operating, and it leads to many questions. If UILE is intentional, and the powerful source of and presence within all creation, what is the implication? This implies that all life is created within and from the Universal Energy of Love. An ancient premise recalled for new life! I believe that UILE, the **U**niversal **I**ntentional **L**ove **E**nergy, created you, and lives within every one of the 50 trillion cells of your body! How does that feel to you?

On the basis of this premise, all creation is an act of UILE Love. Another way of putting this is that everything created in Love comes from UILE, the **U**niversal **I**ntentional **L**ove **E**nergy. Also every source of intelligence is a subset of the same energy. That is a nice place to start, but it is then important to understand the nature and the intent of UILE, so we can define it, follow it, live it.

> *If the whole universe has no meaning, we should never have found out that it has no meaning: just as, if there were no light in the universe and therefore no creatures with eyes, we should never know it was dark. Dark would be without meaning.*
> C.S. Lewis, *Mere Christianity*

For thousands of years humanity has recognized the link between energy, spirit and body. We are attracted to high energy; it is part of who we are. We love the warmth of the sun, the vibe of good music, the presence of someone who radiates joy, creativity and serenity.

On the other hand, we shy away from low energy. Who wants to be in the presence of someone who 'pulls you down' or is constantly negative?

The chapters to come will encourage you to identify and connect to your inner energy source of UILE, which in turn will power your ability to give and hence to live. As Wayne Dyer says, "*Be cognizant of the fact that you have the power to change the energy of your relationships with your family and friends through the power of intention.*"

Summary

- Energy is able to be changed from one form to another, and the Universal Energy is Love
- **UILE,** or **U**niversal **I**ntentional **L**ove **E**nergy, can be changed into matter, and your body was created from this energy, and embodies this energy
- UILE is an intentional force, and the source of all creativity, including matter, time and all forms of life
- Humanity shares the UILE life force, and can direct it as energy which affects other parts of the universe
- We experience UILE as love, connection, compassion, relationship

Chapter 2

The Nature of Intentional Love

The task of philosophy is to describe that which is.
George Hegel.

In this book the word "Love" is used in the context of 'Intentional Love', which is a conscious attitude of directed care, and not just appreciation of something or somebody as in 'I appreciate or get positive vibes from that'.

For example, I may be repelled by the nature of a person, their smell, behavior or appearance, yet with Intentional Love I can choose to see their inherent being and care for that. When I fear, say spiders or snakes, I can still choose to respect their role on the planet, and to capture and release a spider rather than kill it with insecticide. Similarly I can care for the land, or the ocean, in directing my personal resource to avoiding or correcting damage such as oil spills.

Because Intentional Love is such an extensive concept, it will help to consider different ways to look at its scope. Here are some of the attributes of the word 'Love' as used later in this book.

- Intentional Love is the force that breathes life into the heart.
- We are drawn to Intentional Love because it is attractive, safe and trust worthy.
- Intentional Love is a subset or part of UILE, which is an energy, a force, and it is as silly to say you can give or take love as it is to say you can give or take gravity, or kinetic energy. It is the cosmic building block of nature. UILE does not expect equity as its mini-me of human love often does. Instead it operates via the power of attraction, through a

keen natural desire to belong; because we know from our deep connection to the substance of time and matter that our meaning comes through love.

- Intentional Love is the energy that powers compassion and bonding with another.
- Because it is never owned, Intentional Love can only be transmitted or mobilized.
- Intentional Love is communicated through all emotion and unprejudiced connection of the soul.
- Intentional Love is also known as loving-kindness, mother earth, compassionate grace, non-judgmental awareness, the Great Spirit or unrequited (one-way unconditional) giving of care.

Though it may seem at first difficult to grasp how Intentional Love is a Universal Energy, I intend to outline how Intentional Love acts like energy. Love has creative power, as you will know via the experience of being "in love" or the inspiration of giving "from your heart".

> Love is the real power. It's the energy that cherishes. The more you work with that energy, the more you will see how people respond naturally to it, and the more you will want to use it. It brings out your creativity, and helps everyone around you flower. Your children, the people you work with – everyone blooms."
>
> Marian Woodman

As it is a form of energy, Love requires connection to a source outside of us, typically described as a power or force for good. This connection feeds the power of Love to us and through us. When our Negative-Ego resists, all of our programmed alerts and prejudices come out and limit us, which can block the energy or even disconnect us.

Mystical connection to Love allows us to transcend our Negative-Ego and re-connect. It is this connection that St. Francis of Assisi described as filling him with being at one with everything, allowing him to kiss a wretched leper despite his Negative-Ego complaining that the leper was unclean and a danger etc. (A later chapter on *Unblocking the Love Channel* talks more about this subject.)

Love models the forms of energy. It has potential energy, so it can be called into action at any time. It has kinetic energy, it moves us. It has strong gravitational energy, attracting life to it. Love has electromagnetic energy, it affects the way our nervous system operates, and it affects how we think. Love can take effect at the speed of light, and can travel through space. Love affects the chemistry of the body, changing hormones, our 'energy levels' and influences feelings, because it is the power behind our subconscious.

As energy, Love is the embodiment of all that is good, and a relevant inspiration for your life today. Let's start off with a quick browse through historical wisdom regarding love and life.

If we look at the universe as UILE, the 'love energy' or 'life-force' or 'creative music', it leads back to an old way of belief and understanding. Yes, I mean '*old*' way of belief, because what I am proposing is ancient wisdom.

For each of us, when we disassociate from matter, in other words die, we enter a realm without time, a realm where there has always been non-being.

> *'In the beginning this was non-being alone, one only; without a second. From that non-being, being (matter) was produced.' 'But how, indeed, my dear, could it be thus?' said the sage Uddalaka, 'how could being be produced from non-being? On the contrary, my dear, in the beginning this was being alone, one only, without a second. It thought, May I be many, may I grow forth. It sent forth (creative) fire.'*

(Chandogya Upanishad, VI, 2, 1-4.)
written 4-500 BC

To me this ancient text explains that non-being (energy) intended to create matter, after which it commanded fire in order to create 'many'.

In Olympian myths, Chaos was the vast void from which the goddess of the earth, Gaia, emerged. In the Pelasgian creation myth, Eurynome ('goddess of everything') came out from the Chaotic nothingness of space and created the Cosmos from it.

(*NB* I will use the word God sparingly in this book because the word *'god'* is used in so many contexts and carries a lot of preconceptions associated with religious upbringing. As C G Jung said, *"For the collective unconscious we could use the word God. But I prefer not to use big words, I am quite satisfied with humble scientific language because it has the great advantage of bringing that whole experience into our immediate vicinity."* Jung's *"collective unconscious"* is his term for the panpsychic mind that includes all mankind.*)*

St. Augustine of Hippo, in his "Confessions" written about 200 AD thought that the world and everything in it was created from life-force energy, which at that time was referred to as 'God'.

Other early belief systems held that the 'rainbow serpent', the 'great spirit' or the 'mother of all' was in all creation, from rocks to flowers and including animals and mankind. Words and symbols were just that, ways of expressing the ineffable. Joseph Campbell spent his life explaining how myths and legends all point to the same concepts of life beyond image. The major religions all have one thing in common, they spread quickly while they promoted the awareness of UILE that could not be named or pictured, then gradually became bogged down with images, rules, hierarchy and finally political power.

Still 'that which is' continues to shine through. Robert Burney puts it well; "*There is truth all around us. We can find messages everywhere once we ... begin to be willing and open to feeling and trusting the emotional energy communications of Truth from our souls.*"[23]

Continue to look for the intention of love within the religious heritage with which you are comfortable. There is wisdom, support and belonging there. Try not to get confused with the structure or organization and its faults. The journey you are to take is one deep within yourself.

Firstly, let yourself be open to a new way of looking at love. You probably think, like I did, that love is something someone does to someone else. For example, a mother loves her child and so cares for the child. The mother is the giver, and the child is the recipient. This is a '*from-to*' love. It is also a way of thinking that is individualistic. It assumes that love is something owned that can be given away. Yet love is more than that.

The UILE I am talking about is not just *from-to*; it is an immersion in *belonging* energy. Old wisdom in tribal conditions understood that the tribe, not the individual, was the source of love, and that panpsychic love was the norm, not something to be occasionally handed out. I remember watching the movie *The Gods Must Be Crazy* where at the beginning the San people are happy in the desert, sharing, till a Coke bottle falls from the sky (a plane) and the members of the tribal community for the first time experience a wish to own something.

The energy of the tribe was flowing with love until this thing arrived, and it was decided that the Gods must indeed be crazy to give something which initiates individuality, so they send it off with one of their men to get rid of it by throwing it off the end of the world.

Today, Western society struggles with understanding the concept of immersion in a society without ownership. We call it unconditional love; to care without expecting something back. But in a tribe, that is how things are, because expecting something back to an individual doesn't make sense, as the tribe is the unit of belonging, not the individual. Unconditional love is rare if not impossible within an individualistic society – but an attitude of belonging and giving within that belonging is doable and liberating within a community.

Imagine a smiley sort of monk living in a monastery – is he unconditional in his work? Yes, if he loves what he does, because he is part of the community, and all is provided for him, so he can give everything without thinking of his own needs. There are conditions and expectations, but that is ok because his life is full, of giving, belonging and celebration.

That is UILE in Action.

Moving on, let's differentiate other usages of the word 'love'.

What about love as shown in the form of Eros (erotic sexual), Filia (familial or brotherly love) or Agape (charity and compassion for others)? These are subsets of what the nature of love is, to the extent that they reflect the basic tenets of love…

- Equality with the loved one.
- Respect for all existence, experience and life, all of which are containers of love.
- Creativity or the reflection of love's nature, through compassion, healing intent, and love.

When we fall in love, it is truly the energy of Love that pierces us, not Cupid's arrow. However, there are many false instances of 'falling in love' that do not show the basic elements of love, equality, respect and creativity. (More about that later.)

So, can we love material things too, like your car, your house, your garden? The use of the word love in these cases is not the same as Eros, Filia or Agape, in that there can be no equality, and the human aspect is, of course, missing. I am, however, not denigrating the connection and experience to things and animals, but I want to differentiate love of things from Love of humans. I prefer the terms that you are *grateful for, are connected to, affectionate with,* things, preferring to keep the word Love for the energy between living souls.

So what is the *intention* of UILE?

The intention of UILE is to have you return to energy, abundant life and meaning sourced from Love within, and for you to grow to understand UILE as the source and authentication of whom you really are. UILE is your cosmic parent. UILE intends for you to share in this, by being authentically and fully oneself, and this means a life of contentment and joy without life guilt. You cannot love another without first knowing and treating yourself as a container of love. That means looking in the mirror in the morning and liking the person you see. Find that hard? If so, you truly have not absorbed and observed the grace of the presence of love, which is what you are made from and for. As Jesus said, "*You're blessed when you're content with just who you are—no more, no less. That's the moment you find yourselves proud owners of everything that can't be bought.*"[24]

You were created as a unique individual for a reason. UILE intends that you find and reflect that reason in the world. (Later chapters will investigate how.) I intend to show that the major belief systems contain a consistent and pervasive thread of UILE. As you observe the Intention of UILE shining through each, I hope this will encourage you that the message of your importance and value has always been present. UILE is for the whole universe, not just a select few, there are no exceptions. We are ALL loved.

Let's start with the Jewish religion, as the oldest Abrahamic religion. The Jewish Kabbalah refers to the term 'Endless One'. Many Westerners know of the term Yahweh, which is a similar term. It comes from the Tetragrammaton 'Y/H/V/H' which is a combination of the Hebrew words "Was", "Is" and "Will be". This describes the eternal nature (or outside-of-time) of what was named 'God' in the Old Testament, which is the source collection of books for the Jewish, Christian and Islamic religions.

The Kabbalah says that the 'Endless One' was all of existence, and was endless light-energy. (Sound familiar?) When the Endless One wanted to create the world, the Endless One caused the withdrawal of the light from the center, creating space[25] into which finite vessels were created. These vessels or containers (matter and beings) were other and multiple, and designed to receive light. When they were unable to receive the light they broke, and existence became confused.[26]

It is no surprise then that we, as containers for the light/energy, became confused. When we are born we are soon told that we are not good, not sufficient to hold love, and it is from this myth that the Negative-Ego emerges. Over time our Negative-Ego convinces us that we are not lovable, that the world is a rat-race, to fight to get to the top, and that material goods can provide a way to be content. Of course it can't, because the way back is to be healed, to be able to accept the light of love that was implanted within us, from which we were created.

The role of intentional creation in the world has been a consistent belief through all human history. Yet we still typically reject the beliefs we do not understand, rather than investigating them for their Love wisdom. Where there is love there is belief in love. Unfortunately the sources of understanding human behavior are also subject to intense discrimination, and what we were taught when we are young becomes a difficult barrier to seeing wisdom from different sources. For example, God is one, so people who believed in multiple gods were primitive, right? Not necessarily. Many of the multi-deist religions saw their gods as ways of understanding the human psyche, long before psychology became a structured approach to understanding our subconscious.

Austin Cline argues that because of the more psychological interpretative role of Greek gods and the Greek acknowledgement of some force greater than the gods, that,

> *there is no substantive difference between the belief and worship in the Greek pantheon and the god of Christians, Jews, Muslims, and others. Despite this, ancient Greek religion is commonly described as "mythology" while Christians, Jews, and Muslims commonly object if their own religious beliefs and stories are categorized as "mythology."*

Interestingly, it is Greek Platonic understandings of Christianity which have strongly influenced Western belief and ideals. According to Plato, humanity should strive to become ideal, perfect, and complete. Plato identified the ideal with God and perfect goodness, and compared mankind's imperfection as 'bad'. You could say he invented 'dualistic thinking', which is also another way of saying *black and white thinking,* or *intellectual polarization,* i.e. that way of thinking that powers judgment, separation and legalistic division. I think you can see why the early Roman Christian politicized church made Plato (437-347 BCE – real name Aristocles) an honorary Christian, even though he died three and a half centuries before Christ! Plato's views powered the church's teachings on control. Dualism is limiting and harmful, and there is a way to view the world without judgment and control.[27]

In Christianity "God is love" (John 3:16), and the Christian mystics see this profusion of love embodied in every person. In the Christian gospels Pilate asks the question "what is truth?" This is always a relevant question when discussing comparative religion.

> *We are reminded that awakening, or enlightenment is not the property of Buddhism, any more than Truth is the property of Christianity. Neither the Buddha nor the Christ belongs exclusively to the communities that were founded in their names. They belong to all people of goodwill, all who are attentive to the secret which lives in the depths of their breath and their consciousness.*

Jean-Yves Leloup, Compassion and Meditation: The Spiritual Dynamic between Buddhism and Christianity

In fact, truth in Love can be found within any open heart that desires it. Consider some other sources… for example.

At the heart of Muslim belief is the principal of tawhid or oneness, while the heart is intrinsically linked to the concept of compassion. *"My Mercy encompasses all things"* (Qur'an 7:156). *"My mercy takes precedence over my anger", "There is no compulsion in religion"* (2:256). Islam sees the sentiments of love and compassion, 'com passio' – the ability to feel with the other, as expressions of the interconnected oneness of all human beings, reflecting the oneness and unity of God. It should not surprise you that the Qur'an (Koran) says:

> *"Truly, those who believe, and the Jews, and the Christians and Sabeans – whosoever believes in God and the Day of Judgement and act virtuously will receive their reward from their Lord; no fear of grief will befall them"*. (2:62) and *"Whoever saves the life of one human being, it shall be as if he had saved the whole of humankind"* (5:32)

The Sikh religion says that when one's mind is full of love, the person will overlook deficiency in others and accept them whole-heartedly as a product of God. Sikhism tells us that Waheguru is a "loving God", full of compassion and kindness. It is the duty of the Sikh to take on qualities of this nature and to easily forgive; to never hate anyone; to live in His Hukam – "Will" and to practice compassion and humility.

"Only those who have love, will attain God"

Guru Gobind Singh Ji.

The Buddhist traditions are based around mindfulness, compassion and a deep sense of reality where all is connected. One of my favorite Buddhists is Thich Nhat Hanh, who explains:

> *Everything in the cosmos has come together to bring us this table. Looking deeply at the sunshine, the leaves of the tree, and the clouds, we can see the table. The one can be seen in the all, and the all can be seen in the one. One cause is never enough to bring about an effect. A cause must, at the same time, be an effect, and every effect must also be the cause of something else. Cause and effect inter-are. The idea of first and only cause, something that does not itself need a cause, cannot be applied.*

Whichever story or tradition that is the major influence for meaning in life; there is usually an underlying root belief on which each of us bases our belief. This may be a belief in science, personality or religion. In the major religions the mystic streams seem always to have been present, highlighting Love, compassion and acceptance/non-judgment with the whole.

You too may follow one of these common traditions, but modern media indoctrination requires us to look hard at what we subconsciously believe, as opposed to what we espouse publicly.

For example, Sally, 40, a cute redhead who was not overweight, believed that she was fat and ugly, but in therapy, she found that behind that belief, was an underlying belief that love is determined by appearance as promulgated via tabloids and TV, and as she felt unloved, the conclusion she came to was that she must be fat and ugly.

Going behind that in therapy, one stage deeper into Sally's unconscious, it was discovered that as a child she was told that she was essentially bad, and that the only way she could be accepted by her God, was to not make mistakes, lie, cheat or any other variation to social and moral codes as defined by her parents. As this is a Mission Impossible, over time Sally formed the root belief that all love and acceptance are conditional. She also understood that if she failed to believe in an external forgiveness, she would be relegated to fire and brimstone for eternity.

The root belief that eternal life is conditional on what you do, or worse still, that it is conditional on what someone else tells you to believe, is mind-warping Negative-Ego at work.

For this reason, many people reject the eternal, preferring to believe that it is better to imagine death as the 'big red switch' for all consciousness. However, this root belief can niggle away for a lifetime, because the mystery of life is far wider than any single human's experience and thought.

Being open to a cosmic consciousness is by far the most common human desire, though each individual will struggle with defining what that is, and whether it has creative intention. Using a convention for referring to this power or consciousness such as 'Great Spirit' or 'The Endless One' or 'The Power of Intention' can assist in differentiating between awesome galactic (yet also microcosmic) UILE and a human defined God constrained to human characteristics, which is external and 'other'.

I would like to encourage you to believe as you are guided from inside, not outside. Everyone who writes projects their own beliefs in their work. I hope to be clear about my position so that you can see my point of view and accept or reject it as you wish. I have unlimited confidence in the intentionality of Love. I believe that UILE is behind all consciousness and creativity. I believe that UILE is eternal. I believe that UILE has transformed into matter, time and other forms of energy like potential energy, kinetic energy, and gravity.[28] I also believe that UILE is present inside, as the spirit of our unconscious self, accessible via the psyche by everyone.

Starting from that root belief, I don't have to convert or convince anyone about anything. UILE will do that. The desire of my own being is to be authentic to who I am, to listen to and act with Love. That is all. Faith can be consistent in source and yet varied in interpretation.

If a mistake is made, it is a way of learning. Growth will

happen from that mistake, or error, just like when a baby falls down, they are in fact learning to walk. Eternal life is not conditional on what you do or don't do, or if it is 'wrong' by societal definition. Referring back to Sally, if she had accepted this root belief that she is a creation of UILE, she may have been less inclined to evaluate herself as negative.

This root belief of being a creation of Intentional Love supports law and order. However, it is truthful about the individual's position with the law. Law is only created because of the lack of Love in the individuals in a society. A great prophet many years ago said *"Here is a simple, rule-of-thumb guide for behavior: Ask yourself what you want people to do for you, then grab the initiative and do it for them."*[29]

That is UILE in action. Love is the energy that leads to doing what is best for society because you *delight* in it. That is the attitude of living life in bliss, in abundance of joy[30]. It was a radical message to a legal society, which the man Jesus of Nazareth promoted.

The Intention of UILE is that each being lives in an abundance of joy, with authenticity, delighting in the experience of life. When you reach that point people may name you as an idiot[31], because you are enlightened and certainly not living a life of conformity.

Your specialness is always a function of another's love – it is the gift of intention. Without intention to Love there is no love. Bartering can occur, yes. But Love requires more, it requires an understanding of one-ness with the loved one.

So it is with UILE, it is intention, not the deservedness of the recipient that defines worth. Thus you can love your enemies, and those who may appear unappealing, because UILE sees their true potential, and encourages friendship.

Your lovableness is a function of the donor of the love, which is a mystery. Someone has to love you for what you are in order for you to experience lovableness. Without acceptance, lovableness is just a hope. Physical beauty, humor, riches – none of these automatically will create intent by another. As Charles Revson, founder of Revlon said *"In the factory we make cosmetics; in the drugstore we sell hope."*

Intent is like faith; it works to generate substance from possibility. Because you are chosen to be loved, the purpose of being attractive is to be authentic to who you are so you can honor love that is given you. If you are attractive to yourself you will not push love away. Strangely enough, pushing away or denying love is our only volitional choice, while accepting and reveling in it is what we were created for.

Love demonstrates self-confidence in authenticity, that no matter what, you can attract others to love. If you haven't listened to Nick Vujicic whose attitude of gratitude leads him to his by-line of "No Arms, No Legs, No Problem!", then look him up on YouTube. Despite being born without limbs, Nick lectures internationally, is married with a limbed child, and smiles more than most people I typically see in public. Nick demonstrates that if you understand who you truly are, not what you have, or have not, you can be attractive, and shower others with the gift of love.

Summary

- Love is consistent in nature, and is available to and in all.
- The Intention of UILE is always in concert with creativity, free will, and compassion.
- Life is meant to be experience-abundant. [32]
- It is each individual's choice to believe, without coercion.
- The truth that informs belief is available from infinite, often surprising, sources, which we honor by remaining open to.
- Love treats all beings with equal value, expresses empathy and compassion creatively, and exists in sharing.

Chapter 3

The Nature of Space

Limitless undying love which shines around me like a million suns it calls me on and on across the universe.
John Lennon

Space as we commonly understand it is an emptiness of three dimensions, consisting of the 3 geometric parameters of length, breadth and height. However, space is not empty. It is full of energy. In fact one of the seemingly odd conclusions of quantum physics is that each cubic centimeter of space contains the energy of a trillion atomic explosions. These are new concepts that lead to a different awareness of space, and quiet. Historically, wisdom was sought in silence, in the place of 'emptiness' which contains, yes, you guessed it, UILE. Filling time with busy-ness and acquisition is not the same as being entering the space place where the energy is of connectedness, wholeness and peace.

So we have matter which is energy, energy that exists outside of time, space that is full of energy; it all sounds like a science fiction movie. To add to the complexity, the reality of your individual self is outside your body, outside matter, in a different space. Psychologists call it the subconscious.[33]

There is only one subject; there is only one source, one beginning, one unity out of which all the multiplicity of life flows, and to which it returns.[34]

The common word used for that True Subconscious Self is 'soul'. That part of us which has a reference point in time, because it consists of matter, is our bodies, through which lens we observe the existential. Our senses and experiences are interpretations of existence and hence are also in space. So also the soul can be considered a spatial being – relating to, occupying, or happening in space. It is also a being that exists as and with energy, not matter. If you have witnessed the death of another human being, you will know intuitively when the death happens, as soon as the presence of the soul being that occupies the body departs.

There is a conceptual fourth dimension that incorporates time, called space-time[35]. An analogy for space-time is a video that you remember as a single DVD, yet it can only be experienced during duration of the showing of it. The view of dimensions of matter from outside of time sees history and events in space-time as if time had already been played out and recorded and was observable like that DVD. In this way space-time contains the Universal Energy and also the universe across all time. Taking a step back from yourself, looking at your life as a DVD which is separate to who you are right now in the present moment. That is what happens when you die. You are not the DVD. Your life is not that DVD of memories. Each time you dealt with the loss of a loved one, it was a form of death, separation from the space-time dimension. Deaths allow you to let the thinking go, review the past as a flashback, and concentrate on what Eckhard Tolle calls "The Power of Now". As you bring alertness to what is happening now, your true presence can resurface.

The mysterious and the essential aspects of life exist in non-being, in space. Dreams and emotions, as with all subconscious existence, also reside in space, not matter. In fact all that is worthwhile in life; love, connection, emotion, experience; all these exist in space not matter.

The poet, Saint Mirabai (Mira) is the most renowned woman song writer in Indian history, and she lived in the 14th century. This is her take on space;

One night as I sat in quiet,
I seemed on the verge of entering a world inside so vast

I know it is the source
of all
of us.

Like Mira, I conclude that the media of all true existence and UILE is space. So here are some notes on what space is, or is not…

We can acknowledge that space is real, that it does not obstruct the presence of energy; in fact the planets are attracted to each other across space. Space has the attribute of not having size limitation; it exists in infinite smallness and infinite distance. Space is what exists where matter doesn't exist.

Light travels across space, though sound cannot. Our being can imagine, or be present, in the quiet which is space. We can imagine going between the atoms or into the expanse of outer space.

Time and Space.
They are like shy, young school kids
time and space,
before the woman and the man who are
intimate with God.
The realized soul can play with this universe
the way a child can a ball.[36]
St. Teresa of Avila - 16th Century

Space is one big ocean. An ocean of emptiness of matter, but yet not nothingness, because light, love and energy are still there. Matter seems to float as atoms in this sea of space. In fact, what we know as the world is a comparatively small volume of matter floating in large expanses of space.[37]

Look into the micro. What we see as solid is actually a scattering of atoms, held in tension, where each atom has a nucleus and electrons that occupy only a tiny fraction of the space that the atom occupies. It is like us looking at the galaxies and seeing them as a solid.

Our bodies are like this, largely space, interacting with atoms which are also largely space. Even more daunting, our existence with bodies is as one of 8 billion others on a planet that itself is a tiny dot in the vast universe of space, where light can travel for thousands of years and not encounter any matter at all.

What is the dominant feature of our cosmos? Mystery and space. Yet western thinking prefers a recent myth that science is dominant.

The fact that you can remember at all is a mystery. Every 7 years every cell in that organ, as in all parts of the body, is replaced via the constant renewal that is implicit in the mystery of life. So what part of the body remembers as it is being replaced? (See Section 7.2 for the answer to this.)

Each human is a complex pattern of changing matter, held together by forces and energies we really only have remote concepts of.

Between stimulus and response, there is a space. In that space is our power to choose our response. In our response lies our growth and our freedom.
Viktor Frankl, Man's Search for Meaning

To make matters more complex, we know that our conscious is only a tiny fraction of what goes on inside. Most of our existence is unconscious or subconscious according to psychologists.

Wayne Dyer suggests that what changes is not real. On that basis, given we are a changing assembly of waves and atoms in a gigantic soup of space, the thing we should cling to for reality is timelessness, because it doesn't change.

You are really deep in the soul, as they say, not in time at all!
Juan Ramón Jiménez

It seems logical to me to attend to what space is and contains. Space is not empty; it is the domain of non-matter. UILE is energy that exists in space. Before matter, space and energy existed. Is this new thinking? Not at all. Consider this ancient Jewish text; *"In the beginning… the Endless One caused the withdrawal of the light (energy) from the center, creating space."*[38]

Sir Isaac Newton held that absolute space ("container space") can continue to exist in the absence of matter. More recently, in the 20th century, Einstein showed that space has "properties" that cannot be denied – it has non-zero magnetic permeability and electric permittivity, it can support energetic structures such as electric fields, gravitational fields, magnetic fields – and these fields according to Quantum electrodynamics consist of interactions that arise spontaneously out of this "nothing".

The Tao Te Ching says,

> *Clay is moulded into a vessel, but it is the empty space that gives the function of a vessel.*
> *Doors and windows are chiseled out to make a room, but it is the empty space in the room that gives its function.*
> *Therefore, something substantial can be beneficial, while the emptiness of the void is what has utilization.*

In other words, space is increasingly important as a concept, not as knowledge, but as a mysterious void in which Love and life resides. Remember that a rest in music is a space, without which music would be noise.

Space
Brings
Awareness
With
It
Because

It
Allows
Focus.
Philosofree

Entering your own space defines the music of your experience. It is *your* experience, the emotion, *your* imagination, *your* dreams which resonate with UILE. As Gibran said; "*We were a silent thought hidden in the corners of Oblivion. Today we are a strong voice that can make the firmament reverberate*".[39]

With Intentional Love Energy as the conductor, let's make our voices heard, yet respect the space between the notes we are called to sing, so we can create a beautiful symphony.[40]

Summary

- Space is more pervasive than any other concept.
- Space is not empty of energy.
- As the soul exists in space, we need to go into nothingness to find it.
- Deep individual meaning is informed by our authentic mining of our emotions, imagination and dreams.
- Anyone can experience the joy of contemplative space.

Section Two – Subconscious UILE

The reality of this vast, unimaginably open, infinite universe and its kaleidoscope of living colors, is that individually we cannot understand or comprehend it. Sure we may have a good knowledge of a few bits, maybe you know all the songs that were written by Carole King, perhaps you are expert in a science specialty and additionally you may understand how to mix colors for painting. But do you know all? No way. Yet beneath our conscious limitations, we are inextricably linked to an awareness which is of a cosmic mind, a universal sense of being that is subconscious, but even more real. In this section this subconscious *all* will be considered.

Chapter 4

Our Internal Self

Everyone knows nowadays that people 'have complexes'. What is not so well known, though far more important theoretically, is that complexes can have us.

Carl Jung

The Ego is a psychological term applied to part of the human psyche which self-defines your personality. But what is the 'self', is it my body and mind, or is it more? If it is more, how do we get to know it? Who are you, if you contemplate yourself in the now, without recourse to past history?

Of the mysterious other within, Juan Ramon Jimenez says it well;

I am not I.
I am this one
Walking beside me, whom I do not see,
Whom at times I manage to visit,
And at other times I forget.
The one who forgives, sweet, when I hate,
The one who remains silent when I talk,
The one who takes a walk when I am indoors,
The one who will remain standing when I die.

Or, as neuroscientist David Eagleman states "There's someone in my head, but it's not me."[41]

Our inner self is a complex and rewarding place of adventure and discovery. It is mostly, like an iceberg, under the surface of consciousness. Most of your personality, in other words, lies in your subconscious, dormant unless stirred by some spirit.

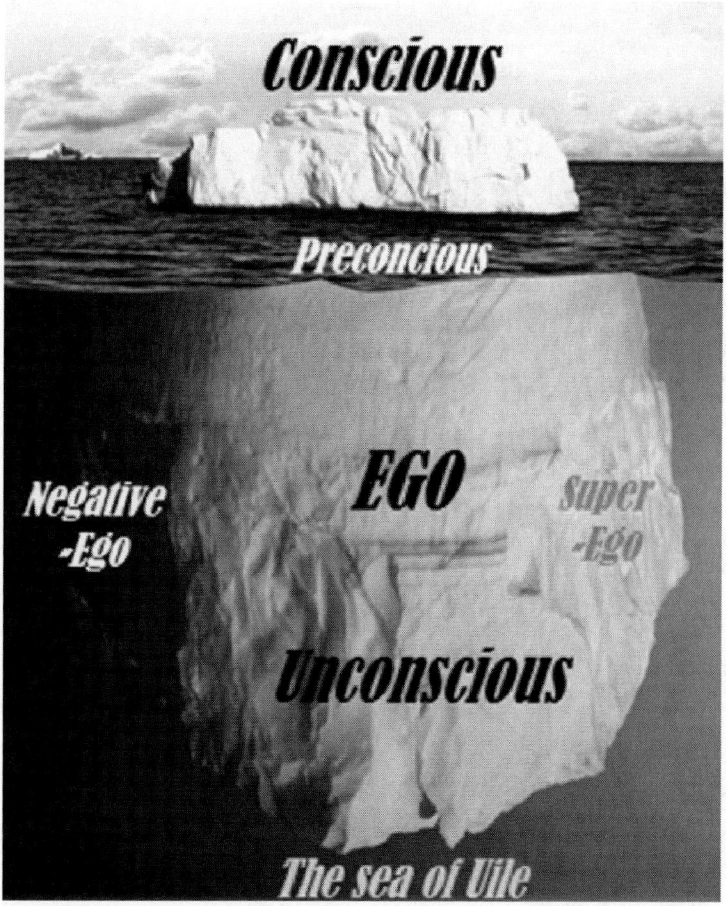

As you look at the iceberg model of what it is to be human, you notice that psychologists view human perception as primarily the subconscious. Their work is typically involved in bringing awareness of the subconscious to the conscious in a way that enhances life.

> The unconscious is composed of energy, and it forms itself into distinct energy systems – or what we might call "energy forms." These energy forms can be feelings, attitudes, value systems or entire personalities that live within us.[42]

The conscious is the tip of the psyche iceberg.

In the unconscious there is a basic Maslow drive for survival via breathing, defense reaction, and the gratification of need. There is also our EGO, our distinct self, our defining personality! While the EGO extends into the preconscious and conscious, it is primarily subconscious and mysterious.

I believe there are several aspects to the EGO. There is the conscious EGO which is what you are thinking when reading this, the center for action and assimilation of the senses AND the attending to the subconscious. Ah, you may say, how can you be conscious of the subconscious? Very good question! That is largely what this book is about, but it will be dealt with in later chapters.

Then there is the subconscious function of awareness and moral decision making. Examples for this are; deciding behavior when there is conflict between the moral belief and a need; (I am hungry, but I don't want to steal) or a decision between rational and addictive behavior; (I like running, but my health is suffering so I will cut back on how many marathons I run). This is our positive or superior, SuperEgo.

The other subconscious part of the EGO is what I am calling 'Negative-Ego'. Harmful-Ego if you prefer. It is often confused with other terms like the *Shadow*[43], however, I prefer to use the term Negative-Ego because the Shadow side can also have a powerful positive effect. For example, a person's shadow may reveal hidden positive qualities. This has been referred to as the "gold in the shadow". The Shadow for me is all that is below the surface.

Jungian definitions show the shadow as mainly negative, but with a critical transformative role.

> *The shadow represents all our disowned, despised, and repressed traits. It lives buried in the closets of our subconscious minds safe from our judgments.*

The shadow is our "dark side." It acts out for us all those denied emotions and urges we wish we didn't have. For instance, if we're prudish about our sexuality, it acts out our "vamp" side behind our backs.

If we insist on always being kind and loving for all the world to see, it will express our other side by sometimes taking over and harshly misbehaving. It is an emotion-based self, slippery and hard to catch. And it is grounded in fear, drama, and competitiveness; it can destroy our relationships if not tamed.

Its sacred purpose in our transformation is to remind us of our emotional unfinished business, of what we're trying to skip over or leave behind. (From C G Jung, Mastering the New Realities)

Jung called this "our sparring partner," the opponent who exposes our flaws and sharpens our skills.

The SuperEgo is the area defining our *higher selves*, right, wrong, belief, emotional interpretation etc. The issue of belief, resident in the SuperEgo, is dealt with in the next chapter. EGO is a mediator between the SuperEgo and the Negative-Ego.

So, how does the EGO mediate? Negative-Ego has been represented in film and cartoon as the devil perched on the opposite shoulder to the angel (SuperEgo), though not asking us to do bad things, instead asking us to think badly of ourselves. Negative-Ego leads us away from that which we know deep down is right, about our authentic self. Negative-Ego individualizes us, rather than acknowledging our inter-connectedness.

"When you finally accept your own powerlessness, you learn to plug into a different outlet and draw upon a Deeper Source" is how Richard Rohr explains the EGO's connection to the amniotic fluid of UILE that surrounds us, the UILE Sea that we float in. To carry the analogy of the psychic iceberg one step further, your soul is not in the iceberg. It is that which connects and identifies with the sea of UILE. The soul is formed in water, it is calved in water, it gradually recognizes itself as distinct, yet still one with the

ocean, and it is the melted iceberg that returns to the sea.

The EGO is also the prime decision maker – this is where you actually formulate choice, not just from your conscious thoughts. EGO takes the input from the conscious, which is an influencer, but it also mediates what we call our conscience. This process picks up all the experience of our lifetimes, both inner stories and societal stories, and superimposes them to weigh every major decision we make. If you have trouble accepting this, consider how you chose a spouse, or a house. Was it a logical decision, or one you know was deeply subconscious? David Eagleman observes; *"Over the past century, neuroscience has shown that the conscious mind is not the one driving the boat."* Who then is? [44]

The SuperEgo is the channel for connection to the wider life energy, in our analogy the sea of UILE. If the Negative-Ego is the prime influencer, our inner emotions and other messengers that arise through the SuperEgo (dealt with in Chapter 9) will be ignored.

Repressed emotions bouncing around trying to get attention are like bulls in a china shop. They need to be calmed, befriended and led away to minimize damage.

"Patience is the antidote to the restless poison of the Ego."

Anthon St. Maarten, Divine Living: The Essential Guide To Your True Destiny

This 'restless poison' is the Negative-Ego which is not working for good, it works against the conscience. It can be called the negative voice inside, or an irrational judgment.

I suggest that you externalize that part of you that brings you down. Give it a name, make out it is an animal; create a way of talking to it. See it as 'not you' because it is not the true you.

Then learn to say "you are not welcome", or "bug off" to it. Recognize the external voice of Negative-Ego when a self-derogatory thought comes into your mind. See it for what it is, as 'other' than the true you. Picture yourself being born. Who were you prior to the perception baggage you accumulated after birth?

You existed and you accepted love. *That* is your true self without Negative-Ego. Consider life since then. Are you free to exist, and can you truly accept love, or have you devolved?

To sum up, Negative-Ego is that process within each one of us which defines the negative view when a positive view is possible. In particular the Negative-Ego is the destructive decision making that allows us to think badly of ourselves because of other people's comments, that says "you must" or "you must not" into our ear when our heart is saying the opposite.

The great 15th-century Indian poet, Kabir, wrote:

We sense there is some sort of spirit that loves
birds and the animals
and the ants –
perhaps the same one who gave a radiance to you in your mother's womb?

Is it logical you would be now walking around entirely orphaned?

The truth is you turned away yourself,
and decided to go into the dark
alone.

In other words we enter the dark side of the Negative-Ego by choice. Negativity and disconnection are a choice. You make that choice. Your true self may not agree, but then again, if you don't ask someone their opinion, how will you learn their wisdom? Take time to listen to your deep Positive Self, the true you, which is created from pure UILE energy.

How does the average person understand how to go about identifying and combatting Negative-Ego? Being aware allows discovery of what is going on inside. The initial movement away from Negative-Ego control is the recognition that you are not a separate iceberg; you are a meaningful part of the whole universal ocean. [45] You are not alone in the decisions of life.

To overcome Negative-Ego requires us to identify the wider, inclusive way, which attracts us to live in joy and authenticity, rather than obligation. The best love poem in history is no match for the experience of engulfing abundant love.

In this book I am going to explain some basics that I have found can be relied on to achieve an abundant life.

Freedom is truly the freedom of the spirit,
wide-eyed innocence towards every moment,
being in love with every beauty
as you cast
inner adventure
headlong
into the infinite joy of life.
Philosofree

Summary

- Our person-ality is like an iceberg, with most of our activity in the subconscious.
- The ego conscience mediates between our subconscious urges and our conscious awareness, to influence our life path.
- There is a negative aspect of our ego, called the Negative-Ego, which undermines our higher self with messages of shame, worthlessness, and the lack of any right to choose.

Chapter 5

The Only One that I can Change is Me

We must become the change we want to see.
Mahatma Gandhi

When I was in my 30s I started my own software company in Australia. Initially just myself, I soon hired a new graduate programmer, Werner, and commenced to build software for the corporate marketplace. Over the years the company grew till there was about 30 staff, and the software was being sold internationally, with joint ventures in Thailand and Zimbabwe.

I believed in what I was doing, and in my staff. I started to imagine that I could benefit the world in a significant way, and hence worked harder, and longer, to achieve the goals I had. I loved the work, and felt this was my calling. But over time my ego started to have a big effect on how I processed that calling. I started to imagine a world where I was able to put into practice the nice things we had developed, and to improve the efficiency of the world at large. I started to think about being important, rather than impotent.

From my observations of the intentional nature of energy, looking back, it now seems obvious that my Negative-Ego attitude needed to be changed. What better way to achieve that, than to take the company into near bankruptcy, and have to sell the intellectual property in order to survive! That is what happened, and I went into another Negative-Ego attitude, that of depression, as I wondered what happened to my life. I was unsettled, though still productive, in a puddle of unresolved emotional turmoil, for years.

Our ego is intended to act as a processor between our conscious and unconscious. What I found was that as the

Negative-Ego in me increased, and my perception of myself became unbalanced, I became more unaware of my unconscious. So Negative-Ego led me away from the true goal of ego, to be aware of reality. I lost my inner self in trying to deal with my outer self. Materialism is not just about wanting things, it is also embedded in the dreams and concerns about goals, the end of the path, the summit, rather than the current place on the road right now.

If your philosophy is materialism, then your faith may be in collecting things; any life based on this sad, false Negative-Ego premise assumes that "the one with the most toys wins".

Becoming aware of the Negative-Ego taking over, observing yourself from the helicopter view of someone else's perception, allows for identification of Negative-Ego attitude stances. It is a surprise to see yourself like that. I am, deep within, not interested in power, or things, but I was becoming obsessed with money, with having a sports car, with being recognized in society. Where do these Negative-Ego attitude stances come from? I have some examples that may help answer this question.

Consider Peter who had suddenly been made redundant. He had done a great job for 15 years and then was told "we have restructured and your position is no longer required." He was frustrated. Then after a month or two he found out that a similar position had been created within the new structure, in fact almost identical, but he was not encouraged to apply. When he did apply anyway he was told a younger person had been selected. At that stage his Negative-Ego attitude became firmed up, he related to the inner voice of non-value. Peter became aware of the emotions 'frustrated and angry', and took that stance on as part of himself. The being of Peter was not 'frustrated and angry', that was a message process calling him to pay attention to what was behind it.

Frustration and Anger are natural manifestations of our inability to deal with *loss.* Anger is typically a reaction against injustice, our perception of how society should operate. It may also be a defense against loss. Just like pain can be a good means of identifying damage that needs attention, anger also needs to be unpacked to see what triggered it. Below anger there may be many layers. Anger may originate from loss of anything, but especially it needs to be processed when it involves loss of dreams and expectations. These are big subconscious as well as conscious issues.

A Negative-Ego attitude tends to arise naturally; the question is *"what do I do when I identify one?"*

Once you have identified the feeling:

Do not do anything to make it go away or change it. Remember it won't help to try to fix it. It needs to be befriended, to be respected, for the layers below to be unpacked, and to then sit in the silence to listen to the message it contains.

Acknowledge that the loss is present. Feel it, feel it, then sit with the feeling (feel the physical sensation of it in the body).

Everyone is different. Peter's reaction to anger will likely be different to someone else's. Another person may see the controlling use of power as an opportunity to leave a work environment and go elsewhere, as liberation, or a celebration.

See if you can name the background to the Negative-Ego attitude you have taken. Are you really the emotion, or is it a message, a call for action?

Ask questions of yourself,

- Have I had this emotion before?
- When have I felt this before?
- Does it still affect me, and if not, why did it change?

During quiet contemplation, Peter unearthed a memory from his childhood when he had been powerless to deal with the injustice of watching his sister have her meal taken away by a teacher as punishment for something she did not do. This memory was very powerful and had formed into an energy image inside him.

When he sat with it, he realized that he too felt unjustly punished, that his years of work, though adequately paid, were not being respected or recognized. It was not being fired that caused his anger and frustration, it was the lack of recognition for the good work he had done, and the fact the company had used a method of unfair dismissal to get rid of him.

After recognizing this, Peter was able to voice his loss of respect, gain courage and take the company to court. He received a payout which he allowed himself to see as a bonus for his years of work, and was then able to release the anger and frustration.

The feelings of a child are often accurate reflections of situations that they are powerless to change. Peter had retained his unprocessed feelings from childhood. Feelings and emotions are ways we can know the world.

An old Cherokee chief was teaching his grandson about life. He explained to the child, *"A fight is going on inside me. It is a terrible fight between two wolves.*

One is evil – he is anger, hate, envy, sorrow, regret, greed, arrogance, self-pity, guilt, resentment, inferiority, lies, false pride, superiority, self-doubt and ego.

The other is good – he is joy, confidence, peace, love, hope, courage, serenity, humility, kindness, unselfishness, service, benevolence, empathy, generosity, truth, compassion and faith.

This same fight is going on inside you – and inside every other person, too."

The grandson thought about this for a moment, then turned to his grandfather and asked, "Grand Father, if this fight is going on inside of me, how shall I know which wolf will win?"

The wise old chief turned to his grandson, smiled knowingly and replied, "It is simple my Son, the one that will win is the one you feed."

One of the greatest Negative-Ego stances that keep us from engaging fully in life is our fear of making mistakes.

This may be experienced as fear of failure, letting someone

down, not being perfect, of being guilty, embarrassed, or sinful. It may come as a surprise to learn that the word 'repent' means 'change your mind'.

Lara had a typical childhood, she learned through making mistakes, only she didn't call it that; she called it trying something over and over until she "got it!" Lara became an artist and painted beautiful work of creativity.

Then she graduated and went to an Institute for Art. She was told that her work was not up to par, had insufficient creativity, and was not of commercial quality. Our everyday process of life experience requires making friends with mistakes, but when Lara was told that her capability was not being used, she felt a failure, and was shamed. Instead of making as many mistakes as possible in order to learn and grow, over time she lost confidence and withdrew from the Institute.

However, Lara's love was expressed through art. Withdrawing from the Art Institute was a trigger for her ceasing to be creative. She no longer believed in herself. She had recurring dreams about art, longings about art, but her emotions were those of depression, negativity, self-blame and lack of confidence.

Several years passed before Lara joined a supportive spiritual discussion group. During the next 4 months Lara found people were very positive towards her, and her self-love improved. When the opportunity came to express emotions using paint one afternoon, the reaction of amazement and joy at her gifts was overwhelming. She was able to voice the history that had led her to deny her gift, and soon was back in the studio. Lara is now a respected artist who earns a living from painting.

Identifying your love of self, of what brings bliss and joy, and then taking steps to go there, these are the vibrant attractions that your spirit, and the Spirit of Love, both want for you. Don't let your Negative-Ego block you from taking the courageous steps towards being the person you were made to be. However, that can be difficult, and we make it harder when we place the responsibility for our own change on someone or something else. "I need a break", "My parents still won't accept me, so I can't accept myself", "I haven't the patience", "My background is too painful to consider more changes" are typical excuses.

During 2002 I wrote the following song:

The only one that I can change is me

Well the only one that I can change is me
as soon as I do
I'm gonna really be free
'cause I may want to change the world
but that's too big a job for me
so the only one that I can change is me

The only one that I can change is me
well it'll help if I understand what's wrong with me
so I won't criticize from a distance
I'll just look in a mirror and see
That the only one that I can change is me

The only one that I can change is me
Lord please help me to recognize this mystery
That the problems of the world will appear quite differently
If everyone changed themselves
like you're changin' me

The only one that I can change is me
My view of myself is different from what others see
I delude, elude, until I try to construe myself realistically
Cause truth lives in authenticity.

(If you are interested, you can hear a blues variant version of this song, called "Change", on my website, www.diamondmine.me[46])

You were made to shine. You are also a person of change, made to experience the full range of life, wonder, pain, joy, anger, compassion, frustration etc. But it is YOU alone that has that choice to incorporate the reality of each day. Instead of saying *"This new job is too hard/boring etc."* change your thinking to *"I am being stretched, meeting new people, this is a new opportunity"*. Same facts, changed thinking. It is the sunglasses you choose to wear that determine in which color you see the world. You have a choice to not wear any, and to embrace every moment as part of heaven, here, right now.

I resonated with what Rob Bell said to Oprah Winfrey during a broadcast in 2013; *"My intent is to help people to find more than success, I ask for wonder in the present moment"*

Summary

- Become aware of stances you may take that aren't really you.
- Seek help to identify the emotions that empower the stance.
- Sit with the emotions and befriend them.
- Unpack the history and layers to allow yourself to shine.
- Remember that the only one that you can change is yourself.

Chapter 6

Killing the Dragon

Gulliver chained

A complex whorl of systems human.
Try to understand it, if you can.
But even in the clarity of light
the image is deflected and
bursts into a prism of colors so bright:
In revealing all the feeling, hands
strain chains that bind the soul in night.

The things that stop us from being what we ought are often small
And shaped while still a child
Expectations of a mother, hidden messages from Dad
and the influences others often had
which lock away the feelings so you think they can't be seen,
In the hope that then perhaps they won't. Then later glean
that passion is the victim claimed
and the emptiness is turned
against the one in pain.

If only one part of whole is hurt or blind
We can find the will to concentrate the mind
to recognize where something wrong has laid us bare
and others feel the same and look with care -
For we are all part Gulliver lying there
the tiny chains of loss are ours to share
and the depths, the deepest depths of passion
are the times when someone crucified is
tied down
there.

Philosofree

Joe Campbell[47] tells a mythical story about the stages of man.

The first stage is being a camel, the beast of burden. This is a stage where the responsibilities of being an adult, a father, a bread-winner, are piled up on the back of the camel, and carried.

Then at some stage mid-way through life, along comes a lion. The lion represents change and a willingness to go past the life of burden. The lion eats the camel, and as the camel is digested, the lion turns to face the biggest challenge of the man's life, a huge dragon.

Now the true self faces the dragon, and on each of the scales of the dragon is written some form of command. *"Thou shalt…" "You must…" or "Don't…"* for example;

- You must never make a mistake.
- You must believe this or that.
- You must not pursue your life of bliss; you must remain a camel forever.
- You must continue to remain in a mode where your Negative-Ego is dominant.
- Thou shalt not break any law. (i.e. be perfect – which is impossible!)

This third stage of life tends to be the latter part of life, once the processing of youth and manhood are done, and the false Negative-Ego voices can be faced.

One of the hardest dragon scales to penetrate is the one of belief. We each face a crisis in acknowledging that a firmly held belief is no longer relevant or sustainable. It does not mean it was or is wrong, but there is a time for all things, for every season. Father Christmas and the Tooth Fairy may have morphed into a God with a big white beard and New Age Crystals, but now they all require inner authentication, and when they face the test, and fail, new faith emerges. It is hard, difficult, at times painful, and certainly challenging.

It is implied that killing a dragon is never easy. Look at the story of St. George and the dragon. St. George was a knight in the middle ages who travelled to exotic North Africa and found that a dragon had long ravaged the country. The people there explained that 'Each day the dragon demands the sacrifice of a beautiful maiden and now all the young girls have been killed. The king's daughter alone remains, and unless we can find a knight who can slay the dragon she will be eaten tomorrow. The king of Egypt will give his daughter in marriage to the champion who overcomes this awful dragon.'

St. George was inspired to try and save the princess, so he meditated that night in a hermit's hut, and the next day he set out towards the valley where the dragon lived. When he drew near he saw the Princess Sabra dressed in pure white silk being led by her attendants to the place of annihilation. The knight spurred his horse and overtook the sad procession, convincing them that he would prevail against the beast. Then he entered the valley.

As soon as the huge dragon saw the brave knight it rushed from its cave, roaring with fierce noise, and baring its venomous teeth. Despite the size, noise and strength of his opponent St. George attacked and lanced into the beast with his spear.

However, the dragon's scales were too hard, so that the spear broke and St. George fell from his horse. Nearby there was an enchanted orange tree which protected him from the dragon's poison, so although the dragon spat poison on him and his armor dissolved, St George survived. Once he had renewed himself under the orange tree he rushed at the dragon with his sword, and stabbed it under the wing where there were no scales. The dragon was mortally wounded and fell dead at the feet of St. George. (Any resemblance to the dragon Smaug in "The Hobbit" is purely historical!)

Some interpretation is helpful. The princess is an analogy for saving your inner child from other people's demands. The dragon is the same dragon covered with the tough scales of opinion and judgment that stop each person from reaching their potential and their true self.

But what is the orange tree? I see that as the sweet fruit of love's promise and reassurance. Notice that St. George killed the beast by stabbing it under its wing where there are no scales. We cannot reclaim our lives by hitting out at the rumors, the false information, and the abuse that our history commonly leads us through. However there is a way to stop the dragon with its scales of '*you **have to***'.

Every dragon has a soft spot, under the wing that allows it to fly. That is where the lance of truth can enter, and bring it down. And the truth is that the dragon has no power over love, for love will always win. As you accept your own self-worth, then the equal worth of others, and have compassion for all, you drive a lethal wound into the dragon of despair. The wings of the dragon are now yours for the taking, and you can fly towards where your soul awaits. This soul child, maiden or boy, will likely be surprised by your arrival, if you have not gotten to know her/him prior to the battle. Remember that St. George had to convince the princess that he would handle the dragon, and you similarly need to assure and rescue the gentle child that still rests within your inner being.

Assure your inner child that you are aware of their presence and needs. Assure your inner child that there is hope, no matter how much loss and fear you may have observed. Assure your inner child that you are there as an adult to protect and care. Doing some ritual which embodies this message is a good idea. Such a ritual may be as simple as to hug yourself; or stand on an imaginary dead dragon and hold your sword high!

Once the dragon is dead, you can dissemble the scales. Take time to look at the emotional damage of every inauthentic 'you must' and 'you must not' that you have taken on. Did you really believe that a God who is Love would punish you forever for making a mistake, for that misdeed, or was that the voice of your step-father telling you that you deserve to be isolated or hit? Did you really believe that speaking out and questioning your teacher at school was a justifiable reason for failing that class?

When did you get recruited into the beliefs that deep down you thought were rubbish? In the next chapter we will consider the inherited thinking that fuels the creation of the dragon in the first place.

The universal soul,
Casting its energy out like a fishing net,
Catches me, a fish of its own creation.
The fisherman kneels, pleading, on the sands of time
Weeping for my ignorance, desiring no more than the experience of my true, authentic self.
Again he releases me back into the waters of life, hoping this time I will not be caught too soon.

I leap like a young salmon, reveling in the light, the color.
Then time passes, and my self-dulled scales reflect the dragon's, covered in obligations from and to others, I swim sadly towards the waiting net.
The fisherman shakes his head.

He wants me to sparkle in the water, to find new kingdoms of joy, treasures that he will take from my mouth as if they were his own experience.
'This time', he urges, 'this time', as he gently releases my youth into infinite possibility.

Each leap, each discovery, is his joy too.
I reflect a unique pattern of the light on the water, and we share the same joy.

I and the fisherman are one.
Philosofree

Philosophy is the love of wisdom

We each individually need to find our own path. And we do. This brings us to the subject of philosophy. What is Philosophy? It has always existed, in the form of story-based wisdom, but we have evidence of recorded discussion which started with the ancient Greek[48] settlements in what is now Turkey, in Miletus, Ionia.

Below is a dictionary definition of philosophy that can also be summarized as "what is the meaning of existence".[49] Indeed, in the middle ages, universities in the west were formed to understand this apparently simple question, which is so relevant to understanding each individual's purpose. If you have ever wondered about the meaning of life, you have entered the world of philosophy.

phi·los·o·phy *n.*

From the Ancient Greek *philosophia,* which literally means "love of wisdom".

- Love and pursuit of wisdom by intellectual means and moral self-discipline.
- Investigation of the nature, causes, or principles of reality, knowledge, or values, based on logical reasoning rather than empirical methods.
- A system of thought based on or involving such inquiry: *the philosophy of Hume.*
- The critical analysis of fundamental assumptions or beliefs.
- A set of ideas or beliefs relating to a particular field or activity; an underlying theory: *an original philosophy of advertising.*
- A system of values by which one lives: *has an unusual*

philosophy of life.

Around 585 BC, the Greek person Thales concluded that 'all is water-like', which his student Anaximander expanded to mean that all is 'Apeiron', or boundless. Anaximander held that the beginning or ultimate reality (arche) is eternal and infinite, not subject to old age or decay, and it always generates new existence from which everything we can perceive is derived. That was 2500 years ago, and it fits with what I believe today. The love of wisdom has not disappeared.

In order to study philosophy, you need to be free to consider what is going on inside your heart. You can only 'prove' philosophy through experience, when you resonate with it.

Hence philosophy is a 'thought through' belief.

It is the heart-felt questioning of meaning.

My touchstone for following a line of wisdom is; *'living the philosophy should bring freedom to the individual, and love, wisdom and compassion to society, to our relationships'.*

Summary

- There are stages of life that lead us into and then through childhood, adult responsibility and into self-awareness.
- Identify where there are external beliefs that were imposed on you, that do not now ring true.
- Consider self-love as a master-stroke to allow your inner child to be free.
- Philosophy as the love of wisdom is the basis for inner search to discover your truth and your bliss each day.

Chapter 7

Confronting Your Beliefs

Life will triumph
Peace is in knowing that every interaction
holds the possibility of finding another sparkling crystal of the infinite, available within any sentient being.
Grace in the everyday.

Sunshine of the soul happens when someone else
shares the same shard of light beaming through yourself.
No words are required.

Search for ongoing presence with those who see eternal fragments embedded within our mortal confusion,
know that interconnectedness is a far greater truth than independence.

Our great calling is to work in harmony with all life,
and the greater mystery is that we gain such wisdom and ambition
only in the silent depths of our own self-exploration,
which by nature is a solitary duty.
Philosofree

"Most of us are not remotely aware of how much we are controlled by our beliefs, even less aware of how unconscious our attitude systems are. We all begin our lives with a set of attitudes that are dictated to by the world outside us."[50]

If we become consciously aware of these "someone-else's-views" and own them as our beliefs, we assume that they are right. It rarely occurs to us to question them even if they are destructive, ignorant or divisive. In this chapter the ways you think you make decisions will be challenged, and another paradigm offered. Then the issue of identifying and breaking away from "someone-else's-views" will be discussed. It is very liberating to know that your own beliefs are actually those that resonate from deep within, from your subconscious true self.

The Bestseller *INCOGNITO – The Secret Lives of the Brain* by David Eagleman opened my eyes to the latest research in the way we think, and the way we think we think. Rather than trying to paraphrase this renowned neuroscientist, I recommend reading the first four chapters.

One of Eagleman's conclusions is that consciousness is merely the tip of the iceberg not just in how we think and conceive things, but in the mass of information accumulated and forming the basis of our beliefs and decision-making…

> *Choice was not theirs, really, but instead the choice of successful programs that had been burned deep into the brain's circuitry over the course of hundreds of thousands of generations.*[51]

Wow! How on earth does our mind accumulate "programs" of decision making over thousands of generations? How is it that we can be making important decisions for such things as choosing a partner based on subconscious programs, and how can your brain inherit information from generations you did not even meet?

The following sections outline a wider archetype that I believe explains this.

"7.1 Who do you think you are", proposes that we are more than a robot computer, that our being is wider than a brain, and our bodies carry subconscious patterning that we cannot yet explain.

"7.2 Holographic theory and the body", explains how holograms work, that our brain is capable of processing holograms, and the implications this has in neural networking with the energy of UILE and prior generations.

"7.3 What we intend is not always followed" outlines some of the issues behind following our higher intention.

"7.4 Belief and Freedom" then looks at why we should allocate priority towards understanding ourselves rather than following others' beliefs.

7.1 Who do you think you are?

There is another world, but it is in this one.
W.B. Yeats

In my lifetime there has been enormous change in how people live. I started programming computers when there was only one that processed all government billing for the entire state of South Australia, and it had less processing power than an electronic watch today. All data was fed into the computer via punched cards, and there was no disk storage attached, just large tape drives with each tape over a foot in diameter. In the early 1970s I programmed this computer, which took up an entire floor, using primitive assemblers, languages and switches. The concept of a brain being like a computer would have been ridiculed at that time.

In a few decades perception of reality changed. For example, the 1999 movie "The Matrix" introduced the concept of a powerful computing facility which controls trapped people's minds into an illusion of life. This illusion was achieved by projecting a sort of three-dimensional computer generated experience into their brains.

Also by the early 21st century I was working with a Flinders University professor in the field of analyzing data in a real-time manner (in other words taking input as it was happening) and predicting from patterns what conclusions should be drawn in very complex medical models.

I want you to imagine that there is a computer feeding input to your brain from generations past, from every sensual experience you have of sight, sound touch etc., including media, and then additionally a source of input which is energy, the effect of radio, gravity, heat and any other energy. What an overload that would be to your conscious mind! However, all these streams of input are able to be processed and filtered so that only a minute fragment surfaces.

Your conscious mind, the tip of the iceberg of self, is then mostly only reacting to the filtering process. For example, if the filters all feed to you that your spouse should be thin to be attractive, how much of your choice is it that you then select someone that matches that model? What if your generational input says "violence is how my family has always achieved compliance", then how likely is it that you will choose to go against that filtered input?

Which 'you' is it that can make that choice, and where do you get the energy to decide to go against the subconscious flow? Think about Gandhi and how his non-violence movement influenced Dr Martin Luther King. How did that happen? Was it by thought, or heart energy, that that love flowed across the world?

Identifying and reprocessing the input requires something more than conscious thought. It involves tapping into a wider consciousness, an intentionality of good.

The model of the brain being the center of decision making is simplistic and requires new thinking to allow for the impact of UILE into our moral and ethical decision making.

7.2 Holographic theory and facts

If you take two sheets of insect mesh and move one across the other, you will see interesting patterns emerge. These whorls are called interference patterns. Similarly if you were to take a movie from both your left and right eye and somehow superimpose them you would get an interference pattern.

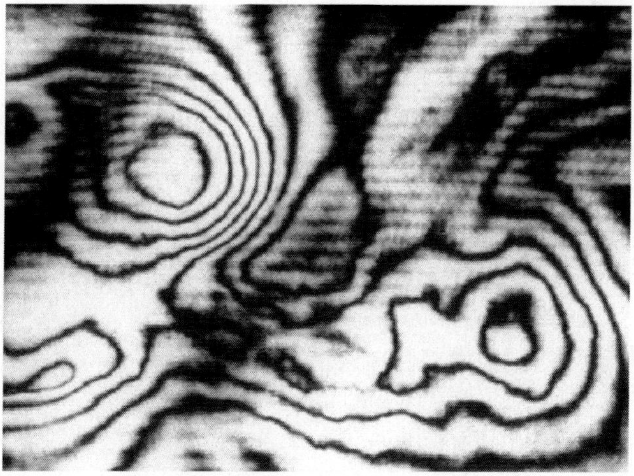

An *Example Interference Pattern*

In the 1960s when two separate laser images of a three-dimensional object (taken from different angles) were projected onto a photographic plate the result was an interference pattern containing spatial information about the object being filmed. When the photo of such a pattern is illuminated with a laser, a three-dimensional hologram appears (remember the one of Princess Leia in the beginning of Star Wars IV?).

Researchers at the time concluded that holograms were probably how the mind recorded three-dimensional images. To do this implies that the brain has the capability to convert any pattern into a wave and back again, using math called Fourier transforms. Is there any evidence that the human body holds holographic data and that the brain can do Fourier transforms on this data?

Bear with me as we jump briefly to the theory of logic. A premise is a theory to explain a stated case. If there is an example that disproves the premise it is therefore illogical to support that premise.

For example, it is a scientific premise that memory is somehow retained within computer-like brain neurons. If a person's brain is half removed and memory is fully retained, then the memory should be in the other half of the brain for this base premise to be correct.

However, in a series of different case studies where large sections of the brain were removed with cancer, apparent full memory was still retained.

Then further information came to light. A university graduate undergoing a head examination was discovered to have a head literally mostly fluid, with only 5% of normal brain matter scattered along the rim of his skull. His functioning and memory was normal. Other studies showed how memory surfaced from people who have had transplants, memories they could not have known, but which were associated only to the donor. How can these facts be explained?

Based on these examples alone we can no longer logically accept that standard digital storage with specific memory location can explain how memory is stored in our brain. However, Holograms offer new insights into how memory may be stored!

One of the interesting attributes of a holographic image is that *when it is cut into sections, each piece of the image contains the full 3D image of the object!* This could explain how the brain can retain a holistic memory even if part of the brain is removed. Holograms can contain not only 3D but movement patterns as well as all other experiential records such as smell, sound etc.

Holograms are also a very efficient way of keeping data. If a hologram is distributed across the entire body mass, part of the hologram recorded in the organ being transplanted could carry memories. This would explain distributed memory and other interesting enigmas.

For example, what if each cell of the body contains holographic patterns which are not from an organ donor, but from your ancestors, via the genetic material passed down to you? This opens up a lot of alternatives, including explanations for synchronicity, cultural norms etc. However, cell holograms still assume that the holographic patterns are being held in matter. We now know that matter itself is formed at the sub-atomic level from waves that interconnect and can communicate and interact in ways we cannot yet explain.

In his book, *The Holographic Universe* author Michael Talbot refers to an example of a dream where a woman working at a Chinese hospital in Wuchang described (and drew) an accurate depiction of destruction of the hospital in a way that only occurred years later, when the Japanese attacked China. Psychologist C J Jung believed that a collective unconscious existed which could explain such predictions. Is it possible that our transmitted DNA also carries holographic information which would support this belief? I believe so.

A leading quantum physicist, David Bohm, has proposed that the universe itself is "a kind of giant, flowing hologram". Bohm also believed that thought itself "is the one which controls each one of us" in much the same way that "The Matrix" writers imagined a computer controlled human thought in that movie.

Indeed Bohm concluded that there is only one 'holomovement' which contains all experience, all existence, and all scientific law. If we are all connected then it is our role within time to remove any perceptions of disconnection which we have.

This theory is not fantasy because it is based on known science, yet it provides a paradigm I used to yearn for, which explains where meaning, knowledge and experience intersect.

Science, philosophy, psychology and spirituality are all part of the same 'you'.

It makes sense that you would obey your intentions and understandings. Not that it is easy. How many times have you made a New Year's Resolution, only to break it in the first week, month or quarter? The battle can be neurological, as in the "Alien Hand Syndrome" where a sufferer battles one of their own hands.

However, the battle about intention is mostly not observable.

7.3 What we intend is not always followed

It makes sense to obey your ethics and principles. So what? In chapter 5 the subject of change was raised. I want to ask a really important follow-up question. When did you last change your beliefs? Never, you say?

If so, then where did you get these beliefs from? Was it from your parents as a child? If you inherited them from family or others, isn't it time you had a look at how much they are *your* beliefs. What if you discover they are inherited Negative-Ego rubbish, such as "you become like those you spend time with (i.e. we are better than those others)" or "spare the rod and spoil the child" or "If you make a mistake you will be punished by God". If so, it is time you started to identify and face your inner questions.

Be honest with yourself, and re-evaluate the motives and meaning of what you believe. You may be surprised to find that there are many questions that are waiting to be answered. Perhaps you, like me, found that what you were taught and accepted as truth over time began to sit uncomfortably with you. For example, I was taught that war was necessary for the good of the nation. Do I believe that now? No. I was challenged by internal messages. My belief changed.

Similarly what you hold on to as core beliefs can change. When my son died, I could no longer accept that a loving creator would sacrifice his son as punishment. In fact I came to understand that the energy of Love is about total acceptance of all people. That meant change, confusion, rejection by some who think they are the only ones who know right, but a sense of humble acceptance within myself.

Obedience to the concept of your ethical *god* is suspicious when it is commanded by somebody external to yourself. The way to find what to believe in is to follow where Love resides.

That is not in commands, but in loving kindness, from people you respect for their sparkling eyes, their compassion, their connection, and their ability to walk with care, softly, on this planet.

Wash through me like an enema
Clean out all the crap
Of judgment and possession;
There's been enough of that
And I want to be free for what
I was sent here for
Wash through me like an enema
The truth will clean me more
So I can have the energy
To bring to every day
a vibrance, and the eyes to see
The old me flushed away.
Philosofree

Where did you get *your* ethics or the definition from? Was it from internal introspection and observation of these loving elders, without external demands? Unfortunately we are mainly programmed on command as children, and it can take a long time to grow up.

You are aware of the childhood game called 'broken telephone'. People are arranged in a row, the first one is given a simple message, each one whispers the message to the next in the row, and by the end, the message is always different, sometimes hilariously so.

In the family line, the broken telephone that started as "You must obey your good" changes to "You must obey god" then becomes "You must obey our god" and often ends up as "You must obey me (parent, teacher, authority figure), as the voice of God". This is very destructive, as it infers things that are false, particularly the false view that God as a concept is owned by the communicator. Your god is what YOU believe, not what someone else believes.

The concept of the unknowable, the unnameable, and the Great Spirit of all, is either experienced via the internal messages that will be the subject of later chapters, or it is a projection of someone else's belief, via voice, word, text or command from someone else, the communicator. I will call this communication of another's belief, the 'external voice'.

The external voice often carries messages which we inherit as belief for one of two prime reasons. Respect for the communicator, which is deference to another's history or reputation, or the denial of right to choose what you believe, which is always the result of the misuse of power. Neither of these is true belief. When you reconsider what you believe, be very wary of beliefs that snuck into your belief portfolio from these sources.

It is not the role of the person that is important, it is their Love, the way they helped you believe in yourself. Think about the role of the following people in your lives. Parent, priest, holy man, pastor, psychologist, writer – would you give more credibility to their beliefs against say a politician, a car salesman, a marketer, a con artist? It is interesting that Jesus Christ spoke against this very prejudice, because the things a person does, mistakes they make, does not qualify them, or disqualify them, as having valid beliefs. [52] That is why he spent time around those who were thieves, prostitutes and revolutionaries. Jesus said someone searching with such a background can love more deeply than the pharisaic religious hypocrite.

Now think about someone, such as a teacher who may have inspired you. Their care and love must have shone through. That is the reason to follow those who set a good example of life. Look for those whose eyes shine, who obviously love life and exercise compassion, who are following their dreams, and who can sit quietly in silence. Read about real life stories of those who are in alignment between their selves and their daily path, e.g. Gandhi, Mother Theresa, Wayne Dyer.

BUT, and it is a big BUT, it is only within *you* that the way of authenticity can be found. No one can authorize what to believe. When someone says, "this is the religion, the theology, or the moral code you must follow" they are out of line. Sure it is what they believe. But it is a fine line between explaining a personal position, and threatening or coercing. Not just with views of the Great Unnameable Spirit, but with anything.

At one stage it was a world view that the earth was flat. To oppose that resulted in threat or punishment. We laugh at that.

We may wonder why, in the 19th century, there were riots when electricity was used for public lighting in the streets. Mob thinking is dangerous.

How many views are there about truth? Look up the internet on any subject, and you will find differing views about almost everything. Mankind accepted facts that are now ridiculed. Are we finished learning about how the human body operates, what is the extent of galaxies, or the genetics of flora? When I was young the electron was the smallest particle defined. Now there is a whole new discussion about the theory of matter.

The point I am making is that your individual tiny reference base within the field of knowledge is not comprehensive, and much of what you learnt may not even be relevant when it comes to understanding yourself. You can be more joyful and at peace when you allow UILE to resource your being.

7.4 Belief and Freedom

Belief is a conviction, feeling a state or habit of mind in which trust or confidence is placed.

It is therefore nonsensical to use power to push belief. Power can force adherence and complicity, but never authenticity.

However forcing belief is such a common practice that you may not see it as counter intuitive unless you read the following examples.

A salesman comes to your door and insists on presenting his wares, and then places a contract in front of you that you are not ready to consider. Do you;

(A) Accept because everyone in the area has one,
(B) Tell him to get out or you will call the police,
(C) Lie that you already have a contract or
(D) Some other method.

If a soldier during wartime confronts you and says you must join him to fight against someone you don't want to fight. Do you;

(A) Accept because it avoids conflict,
(B) Fight him or Run,
(C) Lie that you cannot because… or
(D) Some other method

In both examples the question arises, what does your heart say?

Option (A) goes against your belief.
Option (B) means reciprocal use of power and/or fear in response and
Option (C) is not being authentic.

However, the option I can choose whenever power is used, as in these cases, is in fact to call it for what it is, namely (D) "I do not agree with the use of power against what I believe".

There is a similar choice in recognizing what is happening when a religious leader says that you must believe in a root belief or some associated theology.

Do you;

(A) Accept because that is the way to social acceptance,

(B) Argue or disagree,
(C) Lie that you agree because that is what everyone thinks, and you will be ostracized if you don't, or
(D) Explain that you will consider everything and make your own mind up.

It took me decades to realize that the beliefs I held as a child were (A) (B) or (C) and when I discovered that I have the power to choose, I decided to choose to listen to the universal message that can be heard in the silence. I then chose to believe that we are created good, in the image of UILE, not evil, and that our inner selves contain the essence of the Intention of Love (though it is often covered up).

In any case, no one is able to define the unknowable spirit, as that is way outside any human capability. Anyone who tries to use power to force belief is giving a false message. Freedom requires choice. Everyone, each individual within a group or society, has the right for freedom, and therefore choice.

Yet how can there be choice if everything is regulated by rules? Rules are useful but rules also restrict choice to compliance or guilt/punishment. The result is that to have freedom of choice without the pressure of societal rules leaves no option other than to break the rules, which is anti-social and contradictory to the SuperEgo. Moreover, Love does not require rules because love is not anti-social and never pressured or pressuring. Love is the way, and fortunately we hear love's messages in many ways.

James could not abide being told what to do. He had grown up in a home where his father was a legalistic minister/pastor, and his school headmaster was very punishing. As he tried to assemble his own set of beliefs he was increasingly told to conform, to do as he was told, and to respect his parents/seniors. Was he a rebel, or just in tune with something that was different to those who made the rules? He was not a bad kid; he just wanted to question everything. Every question of authority resulted in punishment or withdrawal of privilege, so over time he learnt to lie in order to avoid the punishment.

Eventually he decided to stand up, and to support a cause that was not socially accepted. He decided to befriend a refugee family on his street. For this he was rejected, told he was wrong and grounded. His sense of injustice heightened and James ran away. He was 15.

Should he have been rejected for following his own path? His actions were in a sense the key to him living an authentic life, and when he discovered this over the next ten years he rebuilt his life based on respecting only those rules that make sense to his ethical belief. He is now the leading supporter of a non-profit refugee organization.

How can you tell if a person (or yourself) is under the influence of someone else's power regarding their personal belief?

A simple and reliable method is this; if you hear a person say "*We* believe" it means that their belief may be compromised. I understand that a large section of the world's population adheres to creeds and follows beliefs laid down over long periods of time. Considering such tradition and observing the behaviors of people who follow that path, retracing the mystical questions is a sensible policy that applies to science as much as religion or any other part of life. As Jim Rohn used to say, *"If you don't design your own life plan, chances are you'll fall into someone else's plan. And guess what they have planned for you?"*

By saying "*we*" there is an association with some body or group, and the individual associates with the body or group to the point that they may mistakenly take on the body or group's influence to infer all members share the same belief. In truth, no other person or group will ever hold the same belief. Our minds are too complex for this degree of patterning; even identical twins have different beliefs.

So associating your own belief with others always holds the danger of losing yourself. The same applies to labels, where you feel the need to be labeled in order to belong. Is the pull to belong higher than the need to be yourself?

UILE did not intend your specific and wonderful being to be a servant to someone else's beliefs. If you share a particular conversation during which you have an 'ahah' moment, then that is great. It doesn't imply that you agree with everything that that person believes. You just agree with some statement or part of a conversation. Check to determine if you are saying "we believe" rather than "I believe, and I share some commonality of views with this person".

Summary

- Philosophy is that thinking which investigates meaning for you, your life, and relationships.
- The concept of god has no owner, nor does anyone have the right to define or represent god in order to control others.
- Avoid any belief that is coerced, rather than your free choice.
- Every individual has different beliefs, even those who are members of a common group.
- Holographic Theory shows that it is possible for our bodies to make decisions based on the experience of others.
- UILE is the source of energy that allows us to break free from external programming and become free.
- Following the belief of others is dangerous, as free will is about personal choice to hold belief, but following your own belief without validation against other sources of wisdom is also dangerous.
- Evaluate behavior, not words.

Chapter 8

Our Inner Messengers

The light from the sun falls on all without prejudice, but it is indiscriminate.
The direction each of us seeks is presented with the individualized care of a dedicated personal coach!
Our inner personal trainer encourages us through our dreams, emotions and rich, unique, individual awareness.
Don't complain you don't have daily guidance –it shines within each open heart.
Philosofree

One heartening historical tradition which is embedded in every culture is that of silent listening or 'inner work'. This is one way that the experience of the 'other' can be known. It can be called meditation, yoga, contemplation or 'sitting quietly listening to nature', and through these practices the universal intention to love can be heard. This practice opens up space within us, and we can discover who we truly are, by tapping into the energy within. We are used to the noise of the world, but the most important personal messages arrive with no noise at all.

These *'inner dynamics'* refer to anything that goes on inside you, any energy system that lives and acts from within you. It may be an emotional event, such as a surge of anger. It may be an inner conflict, an inner personality acting within you, a feeling, an attitude, a mood. It is from these inner dynamics that we can learn to understand what is going on inside. St. Francis of Assisi gave us this inspiring poem; *"There are beautiful wild forces within us. Let them turn the mills inside and fill sacks that feed even heaven."*

Attending to inner dynamics is inner work.

We will now consider several forms of inner work.

Listening in Silence

Carl Jung once studied the aboriginal people of Australia. At the time he interviewed and observed them, he found that two-thirds of their waking lives were spent in silent listening and observation. For example, if an aboriginal person found that they were unbalanced in their self, that there appeared to be a conflict that needed sorting out, they would typically 'go walkabout'. This involved leaving the tribe, the known, and the safe, and spending days, weeks and even months in solitary, wandering through the vast expanses of Australian outback bush. In addition to this, there were spirit quests, dream interpretation and ceremonies that all directed these big-hearted and aware people back into their true being. Today in the western world if we take a week off for reflection, such as I did to go on a silent retreat some years ago, it is looked at as unusual, perhaps even odd.

Yet the allocation of time to find inner understanding, peace and joy is universally a common goal. What has induced western humanity to spend more time on attaining belongings and fame rather than rediscovering themselves? The Negative-Ego has. It claims via the mind, not the soul, that it can offer happiness by the accumulation of stuff. Deep down we all know this is not possible. What do we keep of this material stuff when we die? Nothing. But there is a wealth gained by introspection which is eternal.

How do we know about what happens during silent contemplation? We know because the mystical listeners, known sometimes as mystics, often wrote about it. Who are they? Consider some examples;

- Rumi – the most popular poet printed today, was an Islamic mystic.
- St. Francis – the namesake of the current pope and the subject of the film "Brother Sun, Sister Moon" was a

Christian mystic, Universalist and poet.

- St. John of the Cross – another Christian mystic who was tortured for his beliefs of peace and compassion[53], but still wrote of intense joy: "*Look, these damaged wings of mine are finally stretched full and laughing in delight. Our souls are rising near to you – this earth was the bow that launched us into your space; so restore me into your arms, dear God, like a precious jewel that you had dropped and now you retrieve.*"

However, the mystics held onto their own beliefs without the desire for commanding others to accept them, just asking for the opportunity to listen to their own authenticity. They received these messages via their dreams, and other experiences. Your body is one of the major sources of instruction; it constantly reminds you of your health, your physical needs, and acts as a weather vane to point to imbalance. Listening to body is also important.

Paying attention to the health and balance of your body is addressed in "Health Systems" in Chapter 22. Solitary Contemplation will be explored more in Chapter 23.

Dreams

Even a short, seemingly insignificant dream tries to tell us something that we need to know. Dreams never waste our time. If we take the trouble to listen to the 'little' dreams, we find that they carry important messages.
Robert A Johnson

Mark was really upset. He was trying to establish why he felt distance from any sort of meaning. He had prayed to his God, and got no answer. "I don't understand why God doesn't answer my prayers, how hard would that be for the master of the universe?"

When Mark was asked how he expected to hear an answer from God, he couldn't respond. He remained upset even after he discovered a rich mine of dreams, emotion, and a lack of any time spent in quiet. "God doesn't talk to me through those ways!" he claimed.

However, most religions, and certainly all the Judaic religions[54], have a strong tradition of dreams being messages from God. The story of *Joseph and his Technicolor Dream Coat* is such a classic dream interpretation story from the Old Testament. What if the Unnameable One uses your own inner creativity to generate dreams which map messages? Eventually Mark listened enough to hear answers through his dreams, answers to what was happening deep within him.

Which associations lead to a correct dream interpretation? C. G. Jung had an answer that sounds deceptively simple:

> As you go through various associations you may find an association that touches you where you are wounded or confused, shows you something you had never looked at before, or generates a lot of energy in you. In that moment you will get a rush of conviction from somewhere deep inside: *It fits. It clicks*. Although this method sounds too simple, it is reliable. Remember that dreams are made out of energy. One way to find the essence of a dream symbol is to go where the energy is. Every association is calculated to rouse us, to wake us up. It is organically tied to energy systems deep in the substrata of the subconscious. When you make a connection that is very close to the energy source, sparks fly! It is as though you touched a live wire: the association *clicks*![55]

In the following example you will see how a dream association *clicked* for me.

I had a series of recurrent dreams in the late 1990s which were quite disturbing. In the dreams, I was in a concrete pillbox, the sort of ugly concrete defenses built along the English Channel during World War II. There was only one exit, through the top of the concrete block, and it was through that exit that I emerged.

I lay on the top of the cement box, and both my arms and legs were chopped off, so I was limbless, and bleeding. I felt terrible loss.

In 2000, I was getting the message that these dreams needed to be attended to, so I arranged a meeting over lunch with Rob, one of my friends who is a psychologist, to help me interpret the meaning.

He explained that climbing down in a dream refers typically to going into the unconscious, and that climbing up is returning to consciousness. So my dream was trying to bring to consciousness something from deep within.

He then asked many questions about the meanings of aspects of my dream, such as losing a limb. What did that mean to me? I did not know, so he then started to ask questions about my life, what had I struggled with, or perhaps needed to be brought to my conscious awareness. Nothing seemed to connect, until he asked me *"When did you last play music?"*

At that time I had been working 60 plus hours a week on my emerging software business, and for over 10 years I had not picked up my guitar or sang. I had submerged my art into the mire of business work, and my subconscious need was emerging as a dream. As soon as Rob mentioned this, I burst into tears, which surprised me. It was something that I needed to attend to, and I did, soon filling my life with music again.

Now, was this the voice of UILE or just a suppressed need? I am confident that any call to an abundant life is the voice of UILE. UILE is not a distant Force but a wise intimacy and love-energy that is available to everyone. There is also no difference between my understanding of what is good for me, my SuperEgo, and UILE. So psychology, belief and spiritual wisdom are all ways of understanding the same subject, namely who am I and how I am to live.

This has always been a thread of human experience, the search for meaning. And emotion was always a part of that search. The Greek word 'Paean' which means "the healing", for example, was used in the more general sense of deliverer from any evil or calamity and was applied to Thanatos, or the gentle Death, a God which was conceived as delivering men from the pains and sorrows of life.[56] This shows that even ancient Greeks studied emotion, especially the issue of pain and suffering, and some even considered that death was a release from that.

The study of philosophy, or the deep questions of life, was originally a spiritual exercise within the early Greek cities. The first universities in the middle ages were very aware of the cross-over between wisdom, God and self, so much so that only one subject heading was necessary for all course content including Geography, Art and Politics through to Mathematics. That subject was *Philosophy*. My nickname is 'Philosofree', partly because I think we can do well to go back to the basics of how we learn, crossing between all aspects of knowledge *in freedom*.

How do we regain contact with our inner self, and the Love that resides there?

Obviously we need to hear wisdom from many sources, and then decide what sits with us. However, wisdom is about thinking and our thinking is limited to our brains. What about the infinite experience of Love? Is there a non-cerebral way to get in touch with the eternal? Yes. Emotions and dreams can be strong messengers of the unknowable.

So is imagination. In fact Active Imagination is a powerful tool for understanding the unconscious reality within. Robert Johnson wrote *Inner Work*[57], which is a book I recommend, describing practical steps to the use of imagination to delve into an understanding of ourselves. In it he claims that it is "*in our unconscious that we find our individual conception of God and experience our deities.*" The great psychologist Carl Jung referred to a lifelong process of becoming the unique individual we were born to be. Jung found that Active Imagination, the directed use of imagination to mine the vast resources of the subconscious self, can be a way of extending dreams. In Robert Johnson's book there are many practical examples of how this can be done in a helpful way.

Active Imagination can be put to use in other ways too, a simple example is encouraging a child to discuss an issue in the form of a conversation with an imaginary personification. Most children have had an invisible friend they can talk to, and by listening to their conversations with this imaginary person much can be known about the child and what they are facing within. For example, if the child is afraid of abandonment, their conversation with their 'friend' would typically include these fears.

Let's consider other aspects of dreams. (In section 5 we will look at Community Dreaming.)

Daydreams are universal. They are really a form of Active Imagination triggered by a desire to explore inner realms or to extend dreams. Daydream is a good name to show how imagination and dreams have a blurred boundary, and that both can be used to create a path to our soul that makes sense in today's world.

Dreams bring us into a deeper awareness of who we are, and in doing so convey messages of Intentional Love to ourselves. Typically our dreams are about our inner lives. Dreams sometimes refer to external events, so that needs to be considered, however, "*even when dreams make some direct comment on an external situation, you may assume there is an inner dynamic involved.*"[58]

Dreams often speak in extremes: they try to compensate for our lack of awareness of a quality by picturing it in extreme, dramatic imagery.

Below is a script I wrote about dreaming, based on an Old

Testament story about Jacob. It introduces some of the cross-over between psychology, self and myth, and I hope you get a laugh!

Therapist Dr J: I'd like you to meet Jacob Ben-Isaac, well known in his time as a scoundrel who some people say at one stage was under his mum's thumb. Welcome Jacob.

Jacob: Call me Jake.

The second is the famous Dr Jung, creator of Jungian Theory, interpreter of dreams, and all round creative psychologist. Dr Jung has consented to interview Jacob for our gathering, to demonstrate the amazing depth that dreams can show into our subconscious, using Jacob as a subject who has had an interesting dream.

Dr J: Thank you and welcome to this session. The subject this afternoon, Mr Jacob Ben-Isaac, who we will refer to, on his own request, as Jake, has come into this session of his own will.

Jacob: And the money. Don't forget you agreed to pay me to tell my story…

Dr J: Yes of course, Mr Ben-Isaac. (Aside to audience) of course. (Rolls eyes.)

Now, I believe you had a dream after your mother advised you to do something with your brother's inheritance? Can you give us a background, a setting, please?

Jacob: It's all lies, I didn't do nothing wrong. My Mum just asked me to serve him up some food, that's all.

Dr J: Of course, that is why you were fleeing the country. I understand. So can you tell us where you were?

Jacob : I was on my own, but I have an alibi!

Dr J: I'm sure. The setting, please? You can refer to your notes if you wish, Genesis 28.10-17.

Jacob: I don't need notes. I remember. I was on my way from Beer-Sheva going north towards Haran, near Jerusalem. I'd had a couple of the Sheva beers, and then walked till it was dark. The sun was set, and I was tired, when I spotted a likely place to camp for the night.

Dr J: So you were in a transition time in your life. That could be important. Can you describe this place?

Jacob: Sure. It was in the desert. "Rocky". Not like the movie though.

Dr J: Ahhh, it was wilderness, symbolic of searching for inner peace. Wilderness represents an in-between place where ordinary life is suspended, identity shifts, and new possibilities emerge. So what happened next.

Jacob: I went to sleep. Just pulled up a rock for a pillow and lay down.

Dr J: Ahh. Your head on a rock. So you were connected to the earth.

Jacob: (Looking perplexed.) Wadaya means connected, what are you inferring?

Dr J: Relax, I'm not talking about the Mafia, Jake. (Jake relaxes.) I mean you were lying on the earth, part of the bigger picture. And as you lay here?

Jacob: (Sings) I had a dream…

Dr J: (Smiling in a sarcastic way) thanks Jake, lovely. And can you tell us about the dream?

Jacob: Sure. It was world domination, undreamt of riches, family power etc.

Dr J: Can you be more specific?

Jacob: I dreamed there was a ladder set up on the earth, the top of it reaching heaven, and there were messengers going up and down the ladder.

Dr J: That is a typical symbolic image of reaching into the subconscious to find a path towards your higher self. You were at the base of the ladder, right?

Jacob: Yeah. It was like these dudes were climbing up with messages from me, and messages were brought down.

Dr J: Of course. Did you understand any of the messages?

Jacob: Well, sort of, it's a bit weird though.

Dr J: Go on. Weird is ok.

Jacob: Well I felt that a message from God, like the messenger was in fact God himself, you know, the big dude. Numero Uno. El Supremo…

Dr J: (Interrupting) yes I get the message, God spoke to you through the message.

Jacob: (Excited.) Man, this is what he said. I am the son of Isaac ben Abraham (ben means 'son of' in case you didn't understand) and he said my father, and his father respected the same great dude, which is true, they did.

Dr J: OK, so it was the same God of your heritage?

Jacob: Yep, and this is what he said. I hope you can translate it, man.

Dr J: I will try.

Jacob: Well first he said that all the land I lie on is mine, mine all mine! (Laughs.) Imagine what that's worth. Billions. And I will have lots of family and they will be like rabbits breeding and spread across the whole earth. Hence world domination, right?

Dr J: Sorry to disappoint you, Jake, but dreams refer to your inner life. This dream is saying that you are the one who owns your own decisions, that is the only map of the world that you have control of. It shows that your being is infinite, and the love in that presence will be felt in generations to come. Your individual self is part of a cosmic consciousness that goes on past galaxies and time.

Jacob: Damn. So I don't own the whole land? (He pauses to think.) But I am sure Israel at least is mine. You know, the land from here to Jerusalem and stuff.

Dr J: It is an easy mistake; I suspect that your children, and the children of your son Israel, may have taken this dream literally.

Jacob: So what about the kids then?

Dr J: Your thoughts and actions will affect the world, will affect society. You need to recognize that your own impact, despite your past, will affect the future. Also the rock you laid your head on, that shows that you will be blessed while you remain grounded.

Jacob: That is what the big dude said, he said all the families will be blessed by me and my kids. Cool huh? Er, what does blessed mean, anyway?

Dr J: Blessed in your language means 'the big dude is on your side'. Everyone has an effect with the choices they make. Like yours with your brother. This could affect all society. As could your interpretation of this dream. If you take it literally it could be a basis for power struggles for thousands of years, about land ownership and control, when it really is talking about your inner decisions. Did you get the impression that God was in fact giving you a personal message?

Jacob: Well, yes, actually. He went on to say He will back me, and support me wherever I go, and will bring me back to this place. So that shows he was talking about the land.

Dr J: Your spiritual Landscape, yes, not a physical place.

Jacob: But the big dude said that he won't leave till he has done what he promised me!

Dr J: Of course. The spirit of your higher self, God, the Universe or Great Spirit, will always be with you, and that is the awesome promise he has made, he will stay with you, past death, till you are reunited out of time with Him.

Jacob: I thought when I woke that this place was the most awesome on earth. This must be a place to build a church, so we can enter heaven through it.

Dr J: I understand your wish to concretize in stone the experience of joy. However, remember this happened not in a church, but in the bareness of the desert. The Gate of Heaven is here and now, any place, from a desert to a garden, where we allow the messengers of God, like your dream, to enter. You didn't have to be in a church to have this experience.

Jacob: (Brightens up.) You are right! I can just carry the rock with me!

Dr J: (Hits forehead.) OK. If for you the symbol of the dream is the rock, then by all means. But you don't need a physical thing to encounter the messengers, they happen every day.

Jacob: How? I never seen this before, the bright beings, the ladder, that is the only time.

Dr J: That particular experience was a dream. But you have other dreams?

Jacob: Yeah, So?

Dr J: So every dream is a messenger. As is every emotion. The problem with us is not that there is no word from God, it is that we typically don't take the time to analyze the messages from below, from our subconscious, which are messages from God. So we don't listen effectively, or at all.

Jacob: Interesting, that's huge. But I get it. (Lightens up.) So I need an analyst, would you be my analyst?

Dr J: I am willing, yes.

Jacob: OK how much do you charge?

Dr J: Let's say that the money I was going to pay you for sharing your dream will cover my first session of therapy…

Jacob: But I…

Dr J: (Interrupting.) Everyone, thanks for attending this dream analysis, and thanks to Jake for sharing his dream. (He sits down.)

Jacob: (As they are sitting down.) So I don't get paid?

Dr J: Shhh, later.

In summary, dreams carry messages, then the messages release UILE energy, and the energy brings connection and attachment to others.

It is up to the individual to listen to, record and analyze the dream messages, even if it takes effort.

Emotions

What if a billion people were practicing emotional intelligence? We would connect with ourselves and each other. We would have the skills to make more careful choices by learning to respond, instead of react. We would thrive.

From http://www.6seconds.org/about/

What about emotions?

Can they be a messenger?

Of course they can, in fact they always are. I recall the story of a man who was driving up a dangerous mountain road when a woman coming the other way slowed down and called out 'pig!'

The man's emotional reaction was to respond by calling out 'bitch!' and then he sped on, around the corner, and while he was looking back, collided with a pig!

His primal instinctual reaction from past patterning caused him to interpret her warning as a put-down. In other words he created his own karma.

A second lesson about this story is that we do the same thing every time we ignore the messages coming from our emotions, because the suppression of emotions is also an instinctual reaction from ignorant past patterning. Think about the negatives about feelings that you learnt from your youth, such as 'don't be angry with me or I will punish you', or 'big boys don't cry', or 'don't have fun and be noisy, be quiet', 'masturbation is a sin'. Communication such as this influenced your current view of emotions. It probably led you to reject emotions, and by suppression of them, you become emotionally dishonest. You are not alone.

Robert Burney claims "*we are trained to be emotionally dishonest when we are children*".[59] This is because we are living in a world that has a motive to ensure we suppress emotion. Professor MacMurray concludes that "*Repression of emotion is to stop spontaneity and secure conformity!"* Repression of emotion blocks us from the full range of life experience, including joy and happiness, as well as the abundance offered through grief and loss.

Emotions are the way we determine if our life is in sync. We evaluate our success by attending to our emotions, not by thoughts. That is why so many people are miserable even though they 'have everything they ever wanted' but haven't addressed their emotional needs.

A quick summary of what the emotions are; they are messages that your body carries from your subconscious, through hormones and thought, to your conscious awareness:

> *Everyone has these (emotional) chemicals, and each feeling chemical carries both a message and some chemical power. Feelings are information and energy. As we become more emotionally intelligent, we get better at "reading" the messages and we get to use the energy to move us forward in a useful direction.*[60]

Different people have categorized them, but in fact there is a range of emotions, and no one really knows how to describe in detail what they feel. When my daughter had an asthma attack as a child, she would sometimes say "I have hot and cold in my chest". As an adult she would probably say she felt 'tight' but words are very approximate, and especially when it comes to emotions. Interestingly we sometimes say we feel 'the cold hand of fear' or the 'heat of battle' in an attempt to poetically give some sense of what is happening inside.

Having said that, the words we use for emotions include love, joy, surprise, anger, sadness, fear etc., and are sometimes source-grouped as self, event or future related. Other sorts of categorization include; forceful/out of control, positive/lively, passive/agitated etc. Your way of understanding your emotions can be different to others, and that is ok. The question that needs to be asked is "what is the message that the feeling carries". Fear and pain are warnings, tears of sadness identify and release loss, and joy and happiness carry the body's notice to build up reserves and be present in gratitude.

Do you think some emotions are to be ignored? If so, then you have been fed abusive and false messages, probably from people, like your parents, who were themselves programmed in the same corrupted way. There are no *bad* emotions. None. Zip. Nillsky. Every emotion contains valuable information. Yet even those who study emotions sometimes categorize them as negative and positive emotions! Why should grief, rage and panic be classified as negative? Even your hate, for all the baggage it carries, has a strong message to your inner soul. It is calling to you to be aware of your willingness to reject, it is a message that you believe the target of your hate is not lovable, and this mirrors that you need to urgently pay attention to why you do see yourself as unlovable! ***All*** emotions carry important messages to your conscious from your subconscious, and you ignore them at your soul's peril.

Consider what are the key factors in making a decision such as buying a house, or marrying someone? Is it a balanced spreadsheet of pros and cons weighted for value? No. MacMurray concludes that *"all motives of action are necessarily emotional."*[61] Decisions of action are based on how you feel deep inside, the subconscious programming containing complex accumulations of experience. You may think about what you intend to do, but your action is based on emotions.

Think about what an emotional state does to you. Does that not *'define you'* until the emotion passes? What if you are tied up in revenge for decades? How does your logical mind support such stupidity? During the period you are tied up with refusal to acknowledge your emotion, you will lose the opportunity for abundance during that time. Why do you think it is advised to forgive? Forgiveness is the acknowledgement and release of the emotions behind judgment. We need to forgive our own past so that we can be authentic in abundance today.

Emotions arise from the subconscious. We sometimes cannot see emotions that others see in us. MacMurray says that "We know relatively little about our own emotional life... yet we continually recognize in other people motives and feelings of which they themselves are quite ignorant."

Emotions cannot be thought up, and they cannot be just thought away. So what is the purpose of emotions? Are they just body reactions feeding the brain with hormone triggers? I don't think so.

Every emotion, whether it is classed as good or bad, contains more than just feeling. It reflects what is happening deep within you, and they are not in our control. We command others to "be happy" or "get angry" yet we cannot even command ourselves to do this! It is more useful to advise people to become aware of their emotions and to sit with them, don't try to cover them with chocolate, sex, fast cars, movies or alcohol. It doesn't work.

Emotions that get stuck or are extremely intense can damage your health. One of the members of my men's group told me this morning that "*depression is anger without enthusiasm.*" I like that saying because it puts a finger right on the repression of emotion that I believe is the major cause of depression. In the case of my son, I believe that the inability to investigate his deep shame, anger and frustration from when he was abused as a child led to his deep depression.

But of course, he is male, and males feel that certain emotions need to be justified. One of the guys this morning said "*some anger can be justified*" – as if it is sometimes right or wrong. The truth is anger, or any emotion, just *is*, without judgment, fear or reaction, a message for us to listen to. Would you wonder if someone told you "*some happiness can be justified*" or "*I approve on this occasion that you are impatient.*" You would wonder if the speaker had a problem. As if anyone other than the feelee (the person experiencing the emotion – ok it's not a dictionary word, but I wish it was,) can assess the impact correctly. The feelee alone can determine if happiness is a good thing (it may not be if you are happy hurting someone) or impatience is a bad thing (it may be a prime energy for attending to someone's health). Not considering any experience of emotion damages us.

People *are* affected from extremely intense fear, anger or sadness. These messages are not just whispers, or images, they are shouting in our subconscious ears that we need to pay attention. That's where expressions like "being scared to death" or "dying of laughter" originate. Chinese acupuncture teaches that certain organs are affected by different types of emotion. Lost or forgotten knowledge shows that once emotions were respected influencers, both in the body and mind. That shows that wise learners and teachers for thousands of years had recognized the need to balance and attend to emotions. What makes us think that that has changed?

Emotions need attention. St. Ignatius Loyola advised everyone to daily '*Pay attention to your emotions*.' They need to be *heard*! Repression of their messages means that the messages have to be repeated in ever increasing volume. Meanwhile running away from their healing is expressed through addictions, dependencies and depression.

Consider these examples.

Jayne was a plain, single woman with a steady job. She had consistency in her life, but little excitement. In fact she described her life as 'boring' and herself as 'average'. At times she experienced a serendipitous lightness of being, a happiness that she didn't understand, that 'did not match' her life. By sitting with that lightness, in quiet, she found energy to restructure her image of herself. She had been unrewardingly comparing her life to lives portrayed in the movies, while the emotions from within were telling her that there was much to be grateful for in her less exciting life. Over time she came to understand that her life could be more, and as she reached out to others with that knowledge, joy followed her.

Bob was angry. He had recurrent feelings of anger whenever he thought of his sister, and the relationship she was in. Her boyfriend treated her badly in Bob's opinion. He had remained quiet and not expressed his anger. Once he sat with his anger he was able to understand the injustice he was observing, and to work out a strategy for discussing it, first with his mother, then with his sister. He could not change the situation, but he found the energy to release his anger by expressing his concern and care for his sister. Over time he recognized that observing the injustice in his sister's life had been a catalyst for recognizing similar issues in his own life, and once he took action on his own issues, his sister followed his lead.

In both cases, Jayne and Bob became more at peace within themselves by processing the meaning of their emotions, and incorporating them into their lives.

I, like most people, have had my share of seemingly uncontrollable emotions. A classic case is the grief experienced after the death of my son. Could I control these feelings? I don't know of any way to hold your hand up to stop the remorse, the pain, the waves of loss that envelope your being in such circumstances. So, no, I didn't then, and I still don't believe you can stop emotions by force of will.

However, I have learnt there is another way. And it, like the experiences of Jayne and Bob, is about focusing on the feelings, and befriending them.

Here is a way to expand on what I am saying. Children desire their parent's attention, and that is especially true when they are sad or feeling left out. A child will, in my experience, ask for attention once, and if ignored will try again and again, repeating the request. If still not listened to, or attended to, the child may then revert to other methods of gaining the parent's notice. They may become ultra-noisy, or break something, or attack a sibling.

Eventually the parent will notice the behavior and sit down and talk to the child. Hopefully they will do so patiently, but even if it is a negative reaction, the child will know that their parents are aware of their existence.

I think you would agree that listening to children is a good thing, even if you are caught up in some action, event, discussion or other occupation. If the child is heard, they can then explain their need, which may be to go to the washroom, or to let you know that the house is burning down. Does this last example sound extreme?

Let me ask you to look at your emotions as you would a child. What if the emotion is telling you it needs to go against your instruction to be quiet, because like a call to go to the washroom, it needs to let something out? What if the emotion is saying that your inner house is burning down and you are not paying attention to it? Would that not be a good idea to listen? After all, your emotions are like your children, but they will always be childish long after real children have left home.

So how do you listen to emotions?

My experience leads me to suggest that you sit alone or with a trusted friend and feel the feelings deeply. Absorb them and their message. Work can wait. However when you are paying attention, be aware that while what they carry is true, their content may include assumptions.

E.g. If you feel rejected by your mother, the emotion is valid and will carry a message, but it may not mean that your mother doesn't want you around. It could mean in this example that the feeling arises from her calling you a negative label and you concluding that she does not love you, when this is not true. In fact she may love you immensely, and the blockage could be communication, perception or artificial barriers you have constructed. She may be calling out 'pig' and you mistakenly think she views you as a pig, just like the example in the beginning of this section. Your experience is of rejection though, and there is danger in ignoring the emotion. By bringing the feeling into the open, you can see how bridges can be repaired, misconceptions clarified, and relational energy restored.

Let me share some experience that may be helpful.

After my son, Lachlan, died, so many things changed. I do not think that all the feelings I had emerged because of his death. Many feelings had been suppressed and built up over time. This was despite the fact that I was accustomed to sitting quietly on my own. However, listening to feelings does not mean that you necessarily hear them. You may know they exist, just like children, but not pay enough attention to actually connect with what is being communicated.

So, over time I got in touch with emotions that had been suppressed, and also engaged with new ones from the grief process. I sat with the pain of his loss. I found that behind the pain was a sense of frustration that I had been unable to help with his depression. I sat with the frustration and found that I was still trying to repair the emotional states of others, when this is not possible. As I paid attention to that I realized that in concentrating on others I had forgotten my own needs, or subjugated them to 'duty'.

This uncovering of emotional layers went on, using my own and professional resources, I found that as I befriended frustration I released a sense of injustice that is not uncommon with middle-aged men. What had I lost during the decades of loyal service to my family? I had suppressed my sense of self, the lightness of spirit that is within our nature, and limited the expression of that through dance and music and laughter. So I let go of some of the social binding that held me in that self-imposed cell.

I left the established church which I was a staunch member of for three decades, in favor of a newly formed group of religious refugees who wanted to explore what they really believed through a respectful conversation in our homes. This was how I processed my emotions, though it may not be applicable for others.

As it turns out, within this group I found release from the pangs of grief, and a forum for discussing what I really believed. I learnt to express myself in a different way. I explored alternatives, rejected some, and accepted others. I felt a freedom to believe, and a sense of communion and belonging that I enjoyed. I sat with these emotions too, and discovered that I could befriend the lighter emotions as well as the harsh ones.

However, during the years that followed I discovered other major emotional hurts from the past that I needed to sit with. More therapy and quiet time was required. I found that I had not stood up for what I believed, not in terms of telling others about my beliefs, but that I had subjugated my beliefs or changed them, in order to satisfy social and interpersonal expectations. Once again, after sitting with these feelings, I realized that change was required. That led me into a new life which in turn has increased my experiences and my sense of self, yet without leaving behind my strong ethical view of myself. Just like our body is entirely replaced, cell by cell every 7 years, our personality and our inner being still remains intact, so our understanding of our subconscious emerges, changed but increasingly drawn to an awareness of UILE.

How do you sit with emotions? While in a quiet time, I recommend listening to your own breathing patterns until you settle into who you really are, apart from other expectations as much as possible. After that, when you have the strength to do so, concentrate on the emotion that is the strongest. Imagine it has a very important message to you. Then listen for that message.

Such a message may come as a surprise, it may be something you have always known but have been unprepared to face. It will most likely come as awareness; don't expect a human voice or some magic trick to occur. In my experience it is like cleaning and de-cluttering a house. All the stuff that is blocking your daily experience of a full life needs to be looked at, hard, and then either kept or disposed of. But it won't go away on its own.

Sitting with emotions is like that. By sitting with emotions you are looking at the relevance to your fullest life, and it is a time to have compassion for your inner being. Sitting with emotions will assist in accessing joy and increase your ability to love and be balanced. Strangely enough, when an emotion is befriended it will either return to the state of a limb, which sits comfortably as an integral part of you, or it may retreat and fade as its role as a messenger is completed. Either way, an emotion should not be treated as an enemy any more than pain is.

> *Pain (any pain—emotional, physical, or mental) has a message. The information it has about our life can be remarkably specific, but it usually falls into one of two categories:*
> *"We would be more alive if we did more of this," and, "Life would be more lovely if we did less of that."*
> *Once we get the pain's message, and follow its advice, the pain goes away.*
> Peter McWilliams, *Life 101*

Emotions often get a bad rap. They are labeled 'bad' or 'good' and largely repressed, especially by males. Yet emotions are part of the inner you, and their call is always to pay attention. Pay attention to the joy and store the experience. Pay attention to the grief and understand its source triggers of loss so you can live more fully. Pay attention to jealousy which is always focused externally, and bring attention back to the belief of lack within yourself. Just pay more attention!

Imagination and Creativity

> *The Greeks took for granted the reality of the inner world, expressed as ideal forms or universal qualities that clothed themselves in the*

> *divine images of their gods. For them,* ***phantasia*** *was the organ by which that divine world spoke to the human mind.*[62]

How, you may ask, can imagination be a messenger?

Because your imagination arises from your subconscious, it is a messenger from the creative element of UILE within.

Robert A Johnson tells a compelling story which shows why we should listen to our imagination, just as we should listen to the energy that arises through intuition, art and all creativity.[63] Basically, he asked one of his therapy patients to do an exercise with him, to explain his inner life, and the patient agreed to do so. During sessions that went on for weeks, the patient told an increasingly incredulous story about his life, what he believed and what he had experienced. Then one day he told Robert that it was all a lie, that he had made up the whole complicated story just to trick him. Robert was not fazed at all, and the client was stunned. Then Robert explained that the imagination was able to describe inner truth in very revealing ways, and immediately the client burst into tears because he realized at that moment that the stories he had told, while imagined as a fiction story to 'trick' the therapist, actually did reflect how he observed life. It is impossible to 'dream up' or raise from your subconscious that which is not already inside.

There are many forms of therapy that utilize this knowledge. The most entertaining is Active Imagination which is interacting consciously with dream content, talking to it and making it come alive.

Imagination is tapping into the subconscious in a form of open play. That is why art or music therapy, which encourages a person to take up brushes and paint or an instrument, and just express themselves, is so powerful.

If you haven't tried it, sit down with a pencil and try to make your mind blank, and then draw without any direction or planning. It can be as primitive as you like, a simple stick figure or a Da Vinci work of art, it doesn't matter. When your hand is ready to stop, look at the result of your imagination, and see what it says to you. This can be a very powerful way of tapping into messages that your energy within wants to send to you.

Claire felt she was at a point in her life when she needed some guidance and direction. She tried art therapy, even though she did not have any art experience. In her expression she drew people as stick figures and used straightforward symbols. At the beginning she was not sure of herself, but this slowly changed.

As it turned out, Claire's view of herself had a lot to do with her parents. So, she was encouraged to explore her relationship with each of her parents in a series of images. In the first one, mother was fitting a dress on Claire as a child. She described her mother as unavailable and imposing. Claire was not accepted as who she really was and was forced to fit into an appearance that pleased her mother. As to her father, Claire could not remember how he was. In the picture he was very distant from her. She could only remember things that she did with him.

She then went on to create a third image based on her reaction to the images of her parents: a rectangle filled with red, yellow and green scribbles. She described this image as the container of her feelings. She felt red was her anger, green was her happy feelings, and yellow, her urge for adventure. The rectangle itself, she said, looked neat and clear-cut from the outside, which, she concluded, was similar to the way she presented herself in public. As she talked about the image she discovered that her anger, the red scribble, could take up a lot more room inside the box because that was her underlying feeling toward her parents.[64]

The above example shows how your imagination can help to draw out messages from within via art therapy.

Consider creativity in all its flowering forms. Where does it arise? I have experienced writing a beautiful melody that is from somewhere other than my conscious being, and I have heard many others express the same thing. Creativity is the time when we allow UILE to flow through us with newness. Think about when you find inspiration and creative juices. Is it not after you clear your head of preconceptions, and think about the joy of creating from the heart?

Summary

- Imagination can hold a form of dreaming.
- Universal Spirit or UILE communicates via our inner messengers of emotion, imagination and dream.
- Listening to the spirit involves quietly befriending the emotions, or self-analyzing the dreams.
- Pay attention to your emotions with the goal of being authentic to what is happening inside.
- Our imagination carries the seeds of creativity and authenticity, and should be respected as a mirror of ourselves.
- UILE is the source of creativity.

Chapter 9

Unblocking the Love Channel

We cannot live only for ourselves. A thousand fibers connect us with our fellow men; and among those fibers, as sympathetic threads, our actions run as causes, and they come back to us as effects.

Herman Melville, author of *Moby Dick*

Watching television is becoming less attractive as it promotes conformity, yet the entertainment world gets ratings from being *different* which means outlandish and extreme, rather than that which is 'loving, kind and supportive'.

Entertainment therefore lacks any encouragement we need to be our true selves. Watchers identify with Big Brother participants or the comic-book heroes in movies by going outside themselves into the imaginary or artificial worlds projected. Sadly, there is little commercial demand for the small but touching real stories of love, yet there is an increasing need to connect to the authentic nature of individuals, and their unique stories. As the truth of these real stories is communicated, wisdom and love is increased.

In this chapter we will consider how to unblock the stream of wisdom that is available to your soul. This wisdom comes from myriad sources, including the Inner Messengers, and we will look at how to interpret your dreams, emotions and imagination later in the chapter.

Take a while now to think about the mechanics of TV. If the aerial/cable is broken, unplugged or blocked in some way, will you receive a picture? Of course not.

This is what happens within you when there is a blockage at the subconscious level to who you truly are. Everyone needs connection to something greater in order to have awareness of the real, live stories and events that are happening around them.

Imagine if everyone in your house, your apartment, your street, substituted one hour of TV watching a week for listening to the stories of their child, their neighbor, their boss, or their spouse. Imagine you having someone you don't know indicate their interest in you, in your inner life. This is truly community, and western society has replaced it with the telephone, text messages, media and separation.

There is a need to identify the blockages to understanding who we are. Modern psychological theory deals with understanding who we are in terms of relationship. In their explanation of Gestalt Therapy, Gary Yontef and Lynne Jacobs explain it this way:

> *Self implies self-in-relation. Contact is an integral aspect of all experience – in fact, experience does not exist without contact {to either something 'it' or somebody 'thou'} – but it is the contact between humans that dominates the formation and functions of our personalities.*[65]

Moving away from what philosopher Martin Buber calls I-It contact (contact with things and belongings) towards I-Thou relationships (sharing with respect for the holistic other human) is where self-understanding occurs.

Yontef and Jacobs go on to explain that without emotional connection with others, one starves. However, without emotional separation, one risks harmful intrusion or overload. The tension between these two extremes is called a ***boundary***. By separating and connecting, a person learns about boundaries and self-identity.

The psychological approach helps to understand boundaries and how to manage them. You don't want to trust a fraudster, it is right to appreciate the need to separate from those who will take advantage, steal, hurt or control. On the other side, connection is essential for growth.

People tend to understand intuitively the need to keep separate from those they cannot trust. However, separation does not allow for interaction, and there are major times when you need to interact with others in order to allow the energy of life to flow through, without losing yourself in the process.

For example, imagine you are in a work environment and your manager's behavior is unacceptable. How can you maintain an attitude of compassion in the face of bad behavior, and not lose your own integrity in the process?

The television cable is a useful analogy for connection. If we want to connect to the source of the transmission, we have to have the cable connected. The only difference with the transmission of love is that the Love cable is always auto-connecting, even though we individually have the option to unplug or damage the cable.

That is what I call amazing grace, in that the Love cable reconnects at any time, no matter how damaged we are, no matter what we have done that we may self-judge as wrong or sinful. UILE doesn't judge, it just is. We can, and do unplug, but Love is auto-reconnecting as soon as we allow it – UILE is waiting to flow back through us.

Interestingly, when we are ready to have compassion, to reach out to others, then UILE flows through. We block the cable by thinking that it ends with us. It doesn't. Electricity has to flow from the negative to the positive. It won't flow unless there is a connection. We are the same. We need to flow from our inner Source to the positive terminal, which is external Love for everyone else we encounter.

Knowing we are part of UILE means we can live so fully, so unencumbered by self-reference, that we have removed all traces in the brain that demanded dualism. This means no more stinking thinking, no more giving in to Negative-Ego. It is remembering that we are connected, inside and out, that empowers us with a deep sense of belonging within Love. This is an integral gift of the Universal Energy, often known as grace.

In this state of belonging in grace we see new visions in a wonderful way, as the connection allows access to the experiences of all life, without guilt or the compulsion to rationalize our existence, no urge to judge, good or bad, ourselves or others. The unblocking of the channel to awareness of being part of UILE can be observed in ancient tribal practices, such as being grateful to an animal that has been killed for the tribe's benefit. They apologized for the untimely death as part of the celebration of meat for their own survival. There is a deep sense of connection in that practice that I am now returning to whenever I purchase meat. An animal died in order for this to happen, and I do not wish to take that for granted, as that life is also part of UILE.

The Love behind such connection to all living beings shines light on a path back home to our true inner selves. We are beings of energy, beings of the spirit of Love, not matter/mass. Our bodies are not our true self, searching for a spiritual home. We are spiritual beings currently in the form of a human body.

> *"Think of yourself as an incandescent power, illuminated and perhaps forever talked to by God and his messengers."*
> Brenda Ueland

In summary, Negative-Ego is the thinking that sees us as separate, fragmenting us in our perceptions into isolation. Toni Packer explains our co-dependence on Negative-Ego this way:

> *with separation inevitably goes fear and pain. It has been wired into us throughout the millennia, through remembered or repressed trauma, through traditions, teachings, through the way our parents were brought up and bring us up with them. Learning to be afraid of God or gods, of punishment, lack of love, loss, sickness and death.*

Afraid of sorrow and loss in endless repetition.

We are not lots of fearful robotic ants that rays of light fall on, we are the individual globes built for shining light energy! This is why I relate to the saying *"I am the light of the world."* Anyone who frees themselves from the Negative-Ego can genuinely shine in abundance from their inner diamond globe which is the awareness of their **U**niversal **I**ntentional **L**ove **E**nergy.

"LOVE is the energy field of Absolute Harmony because it is the vibrational frequency where there is no separation."[66]

For three decades I worked in the Information Technology business. I have the view that this business, more than any other, requires a deep connection to people and a willingness to listen. There are a lot of assumptions about IT and what it can do. There is a great episode in "The IT Crowd" where the IT staff in the basement (Moss and Roy) want to embarrass their manager Jen, who knows nothing about IT. She has been asked to give a lecture on technology, and they convince her to take a lunch box along and present it as 'the internet'. The lunch box is of course not connected to anything, and that is the joke. In her ignorance she presents the box, as if it is the whole internet, the audience go 'wow!' – and the whole presentation is accepted without question, because none of the upper managers understand what the internet is either!

Computers are a relatively new model for understanding ourselves. Firstly they consist of a lot of interconnected circuits that internally process data, and present it on a screen. Secondly, today, a computer that is connected to the internet forms a node in an unbelievably complex network of other computer hosts and clients. For example, when you connect to do a Google search, your computer may have interaction with literally hundreds of other computers, just to form a pathway to connect to the Google server that will in its turn, search for what you asked, and then send back a response.

When I started there was only one computer that operated all the billing for the entire government of South Australia, and the total memory for that one computer was 32K (32,000) bytes of data. That is less than a digital watch has today, and probably about the same processing power! There are billions of computers in the world today. The network and the storage scope are hard to comprehend, yet I can say with confidence that there is something even more awesome than the internet (the real one, not the lunch box).

Imagine a computer with over 50 trillion mini programs which form a neural network! Imagine that network connecting to an infinite energy field!

That is your body!

(More about living in that complexity in the next chapter.)

Now imagine the 'extra-net' connecting to UILE energy and to every other being, both inside and outside of time and matter, and retaining and expanding infinitely. That is your soul. Cool huh?

As Nietzsche said; "*Invisible threads are the strongest ties.*"

Don't let Negative-Ego's negative self-talk block your connection with Universal Energy or with the people who can be your community of joy.

Love is available to us whenever we let it flow through us. David Aaron says this in a lovely way; "We can receive the endless light only when we are willing to share it. We can do it only one way – together."

Practical ways to hear UILE

Rather than going to live music, people now can watch and hear the best performers in the world on media.

In much the same way, why would potential event attendees go out of their homes where they can watch and listen to the most inspirational speakers, or read the best of books or articles on blogs? We choose based on popularity and presentation. That is one of the reasons club, church and live event attendance has gone down.

The marketing of media brings with it a false premise that there is such a thing as better, or best, in the assessment of what a person brings to share. Imagine if we taught this premise to our kindergarten classes. "There is no point sharing your excitement today, because on the internet there is something even more exciting, or interesting, or better presented by comparison."

Now I offer a mystical question for you. What would you do if you could experience the very best loving input just by listening in silence?

Einstein pointed out that we all have wisdom and connection within and in existing relationships that we are not tapping into!

Each person needs to bring their own individual offering to each moment, and be valued by the ones in front of them physically. To not do so is to lose a part of human relationship. I am not knocking Skype and similar media, they are useful, but the effect of energy is inversely proportionate to the distance from the source. In other words, as the inverse-square law predicts, energy is increasingly ineffective with distance. As this is so, then the obverse truth should lead us to being more aware of being where we are now, wanting to absorb the available energies of the present moment in our present location.

When we try to interpret energy, proximity is an important factor. Looking within and finding and connecting to UILE as an intimate part of self is a ubiquitous need. Most of us spend more time listening to outside voices than respecting our inner voice of authenticity.

This needs to be taken into account when we consider how we gain access to the messengers from UILE. It is proximity to the deep within which brings meaning. Distance diffuses the message, brings only limited dimension, and does not carry the heartfelt energy to another. When you next go to a live event, consider this factor. You will find something different happening within, even if the 'performance' includes mistakes or does not stand up to professional comparison.

For me, I feel sad that my grandchildren are currently living on the other side of the world. I can send love, talk and write, and I use Skype or other media but it is not the same. The effect of a direct visit sharing energy of contact with them has the most powerful impact for me. I want them to feel my energy in a hug, and share my wisdom.

There are three main ways to hear or receive wisdom. These are Listening, Meditation, and Interpretation. All involve experiencing the here and now.

Listening

Listening is being fully awake and attending to the voices around you. These may not be just human, nor in the form of sound. It is well known that most communication is non-verbal. It is less well known that all experience, especially the observation of beauty, is a form of communication. Think about what you can learn when you spend time in the wild, or in an art gallery, or watching a pet gambol in the grass. Being awake to what is happening around means being receptive to all that is creative, kind, loving, beautiful, expanding and abundant. This is the first and most important listening.

Then there is observation of the intent of others. This is the analysis of what behaviors and approaches are taken by others, what you would like to follow, and what is inconsistent with love. We often fall victim to the most basic trick in the book, namely listening to what a person says, rather than observing how they live. *'Actions speak louder than words'* is the old maxim, and I only wish that they were given the volume they deserve.

A simple exercise here is to think of a handful of people that you look up to, admire and are your role models. Who you choose speaks a lot about who you yourself are, what you aspire to be. Ask yourself, *"Will these people still be my role models when I am facing my last breath?"* If so, then your choice is probably not influenced by Negative-Ego. The people who are vibrant, able to face difficult times and yet flourish with meaning and purpose, those who can have fun yet in the next instant be fully attentive to your deep needs, these are the ones who have learnt about abundance of UILE.

When I first tried to choose a set of people who I wanted to model after, they were historical figures. I struggled to find a handful of people that I knew and that I felt showed the intentions of love in a way I could relate to. Over time, though, I have found that more and more such aware people have entered my life, so don't be alarmed if you initially find it difficult, as you learn more about UILE inside yourself, so you will find it easier to discern where the energy resides outside.

Wayne Dyer says *"Every thought you have can be energetically calibrated, along with its impact on your body and your environment"*. Have you considered how you can become a positive, energetic and abundant model for those around you?

The final aspect of listening, and probably the least important, is using your ears, hearing words, and interpreting them. I know this is usually the most common use of the word 'listening', but it is also the most fraught with danger. It is the weapon of choice of Negative-Ego. The Christian texts warn us to *"Stay clear of pious talk that is only talk. Words are not mere words, you know. If they're not backed by a godly life, they accumulate as poison in the soul."*[67]

The mirror of this is of course what you say, what comes out of your mouth. Observe yourself when you talk. At the point you speak, you are typically not in control of the words, even if you have practiced them. What comes out may be subconscious – for example when you are angry and say things you never intended when you started the conversation. Words are a flow of both conscious and subconscious. What I recommend is to be aware of how much you say that is not what you are thinking.

Consequently when you *are* listening the reverse applies, how do you open your heart to listen to what is not being said. For example, you see a browbeaten woman coughing and cowering in the presence of an abusive man. If she says that she is happy and well, how do you interpret that in the light of the non-verbal cues she is sending? The risk with this approach is that you interpret incorrectly. There is no simple answer to listening other than to concentrate on the person with your heart.

The master Jesus said, "*what comes out of the mouth gets its start in the heart.*" That applies to both negative and positive. It is from your heart, your higher self, that you generate encouraging compliments and empathetic statements.

On the other hand, if you find yourself saying things that you would not want your children hearing, then this is a clear message to you to be curious about why you are not practicing what you preach. Such hypocritical words are an expression of Negative-Ego control, and that you have an internal conflict that needs resolution. You probably don't feel at peace within yourself. This is where meditation comes in.

Meditation

Meditation or contemplation, in the context in which I am referring to it here, means thoughtless awareness, a state where the conscious ego and the Negative-Ego are disabled, so that instead of thinking, you are open to who you truly are, being part of UILE.

To be clear, meditation is absorbing the Energy of UILE in whatever method works for you. This typically involves silence, but does not have to. Meditation is *not* mental concentration, exercises or body positions, mental effort or strain, and it is nothing to do with spasms, seeing colors or any other external locus of control.

The purpose of listening in silence or similar practices of attending to your inner subconscious, is to become more aware of who you truly are. By contemplating the presence of UILE within, you will raise your own energy levels, become more aware of your potential, and source energy to give compassion and love to others. These are the objectives of meditation or contemplation.

When you do sit with your inner self, allowing yourself to face your own being, you will commonly discover that you have a wild and adventurous future outlined to you via the Inner Messengers. It is then that you will need to know how to interpret, to *'listen to'*, these Inner Messages.

Interpretation

In the last chapter the Inner Messengers, Dreams, Emotions and Imagination were discussed. Interpretation is getting some grasp of how to absorb the messages that are available from these sources.

Let's start off with how people interpret dreams, though the process I will introduce also applies to emotions, intuition and imagination.

There are thousands of sources on the internet that will tell you what symbols within dreams mean. I don't wish to put them down; they may be useful at times because there is a connection between all human experiences which show through common dream archetypes[68]. However, in my experience the objective is to listen to your inner self, so the first guideline is to be open to what is happening within.

Find a place where you are not distracted, where you can actually listen without other voices interfering. I think that media (TV and radio etc.) should be off, or if you have no control over that, minimized as much as possible. Plonk yourself down where there is at least something of beauty and nature. If you have no access to a garden, find a pot plant. If you have no art, get your dog to sit with you. He will understand, as all animals do.

Now consider the dream, imagining, or emotion that has triggered this. I can share an example that may help, if you like? Yesterday morning I had a dream that I was abducted by three men, taken in my own car to some unknown fate that I did not want. I was in the front seat next to the driver, unbound, but I did not have access to my phone to call the police. I was being driven on a highway towards a city, and there was a median strip between the incoming and outgoing traffic lanes, with trees and shrubs between. I observed flashing lights coming toward us on the opposite lane, so, knowing that I was in the 'death seat' I asked for a pillow and was handed one from the backseat men. I then raised the pillow to protect my head, and lowering myself into the space in front of my seat, I grabbed the steering wheel with both hands and pulled the car into the oncoming traffic. The car rolled and at that point I woke.

Step one – Sit with the input and wait for what is strong in the imagery

I did sit with this, and found that the most compelling part of the dream was the action I took to wrench the wheel, in order to take control from the driver.

Step two – Identify the associated feelings

How does this feel? Try not to think or process with your mind, because you are trying to identify what is happening beneath your consciousness. Identify any emotion that is associated. If your step one was an emotion, try to look behind it to see if there is another emotion there as well. For example in my case there was a great sense of relief when I pulled on the steering wheel, despite the danger involved. Behind that was another emotional state, the frustration of being abducted and under someone else's control, and anger at the injustice of it.

The message of my dream was that something in my life was unjust, unfairly out of my control, and I needed to take steps to regain my authentic self.

Step three – Reconsider the trigger

There may be more than one message. Sit with what you have just identified, and run through the input once again. Was the dream just about this, was my life purpose being abducted, did it sit well within me to conclude that I needed to take action to reclaim my sense of self. It did. The dream didn't offer more paths, but it could have.

Step four – Look for a positive outcome

It is all very well to find a message, but what is the point, how can this help you live more happily, more authentically?

This step leads to finding a positive action that you are called towards.

In my case it meant identifying where I was being diminished, then standing up to reclaim my sense of self. The positive has been in the relief of applying that, and not kowtowing to someone else's controlling behavior.

It is worth noting though, that we are often inclined to react to emotional awareness with Negative-Ego thinking. Remember that any action that is positive should increase the energy not only within yourself, but in the people with whom you have to deal to apply the outcome. Respect, encouragement and clarity should be communicated. Avoid triggering a negative outcome in someone else. For example, I did not use power tactics to confront the people who were in the real driver's seat, despite the dream having me pull the wheel from the driver. I learned within myself to not be abducted in the first place.

These are my ideas, but in the later chapter on dream stories (Section 4) Robert Johnson's alternative 4-step approach is also provided. You may come up with your own way; these are just suggested approaches in case you are stuck.

Now let us consider what to do when someone unsettles you.

This means in other words that the presence of someone brings emotions to bear, you feel different. Let's say you feel uncomfortable with someone, your intuition tells you that you should not be spending time with them. This is another form of hearing a message. Like the ancient knowledge of listening to your body when you feel that you should or should not eat something in particular, this is a way of attending to something that you cannot explain. So listen to the message, especially if it keeps repeating. Where possible distance yourself, if you feel in danger and cannot leave, try to bring someone else into the situation. Intuition is quite well researched these days, if you find you are having intuitive guidance often, it may be that you have a gift that would be worth reading more about. Don't be afraid of it.

The concept of UILE can help with this, because if you accept the paradigm that the Holy (whole) Spirit is part of all, then there is nothing to be afraid of. There is no outside white-haired punishment man who demands perfection. There is just a presence inside you, and everything, of Love, intentional, with unlimited energy to perform with ease what we see as miracles.

In order to apply interpretative action with wisdom, I recommend that you form an alliance with a person you respect, to consider alternative optimal action paths before jumping with a frying pan into another fire. The next section deals with how to live a life that respects UILE.

Summary

- Love is always available.
- Each individual can block love.
- We unblock the communication of love by playing it forward.
- We were made for friendship, to give and to receive in acceptance of who we truly are.
- There is a way to harvest 'right action' by being open to

UILE messages and by acting with compassion.

- Be aware of subconscious messages and don't ignore them, be curious about them, befriend them, and hence respect them.

Section Three – Living with UILE

How do we live ethical lives of abundance with intentional love energy? In this section the paradoxes of heaven now, loving both friends and enemies, while peace and pain are balanced and included.

Chapter 10

Honeymoon Heaven Here

Get informed. Get outraged. Get inspired. Get active.
Anita Roddick

The Honeymoon Effect – the science of creating heaven on earth by Bruce Lipton asserts that if we use the 50 trillion cells that live harmoniously in every healthy human body as a model, living humans can create a 'super organism' called humanity that can heal our planet.

He states that 95% of our time is spent running according to old tapes and learnt habits, and only 5% is spent being attentive to our spirit and the spirit of love.

But he also said that when we are 'in love', research shows this percentage almost entirely flips around, that 90% of our time is attending to making love, and creating heaven on earth.

So we find brief moments of joy while on our honeymoon, we likely will stay in our 'honeymoon' attitude for a while, trying to reassure ourselves by someone else's close attention and care. Then we revert back to our ingrained beliefs and habits, at which point we lose our way again, trading the sublime present for the stressed and dishonest residence of the past or the future.

But do we *intentionally break up* this honeymoon state of bliss, really? I don't think so, yet something happens. Something within us all that is universal. *Change.*

YOU change. You start to see things from a different perspective, and choose to put down the good aspects of your partner.

For example, during the honeymoon reactions may arise about characteristics of our spouse that we had ignored previously, or what was longed for prior to the honeymoon becomes the norm, and is undervalued or even disrespected.

As things change in life there are two paths, accept or reject reality. Identifying reality is primarily observing people as they are. Including yourself. You may have unrealistically assessed the person you are in relationship with. But if so, how do you know that you won't do the same thing again, at the other end of the spectrum?

Typical human reaction is to do just that, either accept what is life-draining, or reject what is life-giving. Good relationships sit in tension in the middle of reality.

If you are in a life-draining relationship; the typical response is to over-react or experience the frog-boiling effect.

Frog-boiling defined; if you put a frog into a pot of boiling water it will jump out, however if you put a frog into a pot of cold water and gradually raise the temperature, it will sit there until it dies from the heat.

A relationship, a career or any part of life that is now bliss can become gradually toxic, as the 'temperature' of the setting changes. For example, have you ever stayed in a job that was bad for you, but it was 'normal' bad? Our emotions and dreams will inform us that the temperature is rising, but we are the ones who need to move, to recognize the hot water we are in, as life happens around us.

You would think we would jump if we knew we were in danger of boiling to death. The interesting thing about this analogy, though, is that in relationship, the hot water is usually heated by the participants, and as a participant you raise the temperature too! Your boss, spouse, or child is not inherently bad. Neither are you! But over time as we forget the Law of Attraction, we blame or shove emotional responsibility to the other party. That boils the water, for sure!

Getting the temperature down is fairly simple. Look at what you yourself are doing in the relationship to be attractive. Spend your energy being attractive rather than in jumping out, or raising the temperature. Being attractive lowers the temperature. Of course I am not talking about physical appearance, being attractive is about a mixture of compassion and positive thinking.

If you see good things in everything, even suffering, then your attitude will be tuned to positive. That means your mood will lighten and others will be attracted to that. In a relationship there is another person to give positive encouragement to, and when that person provides positive feedback it continues the cycle. Negativity is the opposite.

Thomas Troward, an English judge in India in the early part of the 20th century, wrote "the action of Mind plants that nucleus which, if allowed to grow undisturbed, will eventually attract to itself all the conditions necessary for its manifestation in outward visible form." This is the positive thinking part of the Law of Attraction, and is important; however it is a lesser value of attraction compared with the action of UILE which, if expressed through compassion, will eventually attract the relationships necessary for inner peace and joy.

The Tao says "*All things and beings will eventually return to the original source. This is called 'peace.' Peace means returning to one's original nature.*"

Many people express desire to experience this presence of peace. This is because anyone who is in harmony with their original nature of being, loves what they do, and has compassion, is at peace. Being at peace within your self is attractive. Consider the Dalai Lama as an example of someone that people like to be in the presence of, because he shines with internal peace.

If you are having trouble with a relationship, let me ask you this, would the relationship change if you experienced authentic change in your partner? Imagine observing that they are now at peace with themselves, not under control of any addiction, that they show compassion and are mostly positive. Would that change your view of your partner?

Now reflect on yourself. What if *you* take on these attributes?

Is it likely that other people will now want to be in your presence? Yes. That is the Law of Attraction as I see it. Forget about attracting money or goods, this is about attracting joy, belonging and peace.

Lipton, Burney and Rohr agree that the subconscious gunk which we collect while growing up, the programming we are subjected to, negative self-talk from the Negative-Ego, all affect the decisions we make. We bring this gunk into our relationships with other people too, when we look for them to complete us, and while we sit in this gunk we are never satisfied.

How do you get out? I recommend two books that address ways to get out from under the influence of others, and become free. Both are based on the 12-step program for recovering addiction.

The first is Fr. Richard Rohr, ('We do not think ourselves into new ways of living, we live ourselves into new ways of thinking.'), whose book *Breathing Under Water: Spirituality and the Twelve Steps* leads through the process of change.

Here is a sample: (Italics are copied from the originals.)

> We all take our own pattern of thinking as normative, logical, and surely true, even when it does not fully compute. We keep doing the same thing over and over again, even if it is not working for us. That is the self-destructive, even 'demonic', nature of all addiction and of the mind in particular. *We think we are our thinking, and we even take that thinking as utterly 'true', which removes us at least two steps from reality itself.* We really are our own worst enemies, and salvation is primarily from ourselves. It seems humans would rather die than change or admit that they are mistaken.

The second comes from a recovering alcoholic, Robert Burney, who wrote *Codependence/The Dance of Wounded Souls* in order to share his experience of how to get out of this dilemma.

Here is a sample:

> *On an emotional level the dance of Recovery is owning and honoring the emotional wounds so that we can release the grief energy – the pain, rage, terror, and shame that is driving us.*
>
> *That shame is toxic, and it is not ours – it never was!*
>
> *We did nothing to be ashamed of – we were just little kids. Just as our parents were little kids when they were wounded and shamed, and their parents before them, etc., etc. This is shame about being human that has been passed down from generation to generation.*

The Universal Energy of UILE comes as wings to surround our inner children, and to include us back into itself. This is the true honeymoon effect, that we can feel good about life, know how to live our role within UILE, and be abundant in reflection of creativity and joy.

Summary

- Considering what creates bliss for us is important.
- Change yourself to be attractive via inner qualities of compassion, peace and positive attitude.
- Once you are attractive in this way life will respond in kind.
- Abundance and joy are part of your role to model heaven on earth.
- You are human, and no human can live abundance while shamed.

Chapter 11

All You Need is Love

When He touches me
I clutch the sky's sheets,
the way other
lovers
do
the earth's weave
of clay.

Any real ecstasy is a sign
you are moving
in the right
direction,
don't let any prude tell you otherwise.
St. Teresa of Avila[69]

Here is an example of attending to emotion, and finding something really interesting from the subconscious as a result:

I was at a gathering during the pre-Christmas advent season, and a prayer of joy was read out, from Mary, the mother of Jesus. The way it was phrased initially sounded to me like she was praying to some external human-like power-hungry God and for some reason this angered me. You see, for me UILE is so inclusive, and I agree with the explanation that Richard Rohr gives: "*the goal of mysticism is divine union*—union with what is, with the moment, with yourself, with the Divine, which means the heart of everything."

It seemed to me that this young Jewish girl was probably brainwashed into approaching God as a person, which seemed to me demeaning to God and to Mary.

The evening had space for silence, and in the silence I discovered something surprising. Mary's prayer was about having the spirit of Jesus inside of her, as she was pregnant with Jesus. In her faith, God was present in the form of a baby. This image was attractively intimate, inclusive, non-macho, non-power based to me.

The concept of Externalization of god flipped within me to understand the internalization of UILE within Mary. Mary's prayer was not demeaning; instead here was the model for what I believe, namely that God is present as UILE within each of us, irrespective of whether we are a poor Jewish peasant girl, or a national prime minister. Once I understood and sat in silence with my anger, it dissolved, and a totally new emotion, of acceptance and joy, emerged. Yet if I had not sat with the anger, next time I read Mary's prayer, if at all, I likely would have associated it with the anger I felt, and repeated the process.

Negative-Ego wants the negative to win. UILE, the amniotic fluid of all life, wants to build up our awareness of who we are, with the expectation that we will live abundantly.

> *To say that I am made in the image of God is to say that love is the reason for my existence, for God is love. Love is my true character. Love is my name.*
>
> Thomas Merton. *New Seeds of Contemplation* (New York: New Dimensions Press, 1961): 60

Love lives within everyone. The Beatles wrote "*All you need is love*" as a result of comparing their incredible fame with the spiritual peace they sought with swamis in India. They had a point. All we truly desire is love, though our Negative-Ego often takes over and insists that we will starve, or die of exposure, if we don't get the material things Negative-Ego says we need.

Malcolm Muggeridge once said, "The most terrible thing about materialism, even more terrible than its proneness to violence, is its boredom, from which sex, alcohol, drugs, all devices for putting out the accusing light of reason and suppressing the unrealizable aspirations of love, offer a prospect of deliverance."

So what happens within us that leads us to abandon the Love that we most desire, replacing it with the slavery of 'stuff and money to buy it'? It is an internal redirection of our thoughts. Negative-Ego tries to convince us that the easy path to happiness is to achieve material goals. But it doesn't work. Never has.

Spirits soar on the adventure that is unearthing the truth about yourself, both your SuperEgo and your Negative-Ego. Unearthing such understandings from emotions, dreams, imagination; this is where the adventure really takes place, and the unusual thing is that as the subconscious is revealed and accepted, life on earth becomes joyful and meaningful, and the material world in all its ugliness and beauty becomes a personal rainbow. That is the "Honeymoon Effect" outlined in the prior chapter.

Consider respected leaders of the world – Gandhi, Nelson Mandela, Mother Theresa, Martin Luther King, The Dalai Lama, Laozi etc. – what differentiated them? Peace, compassion, nonviolence, love.

Their lives were full of suffering from which wisdom was an outcome. They could have chosen to be depressed and given up but instead they looked for, and found, love in the ugly, the rejected and the weak. Jesus did too, and died forgiving those who killed him.

UILE doesn't punish, because punishment is always applied from the mistaken assumption that it will affect behavior positively. "*A good punishment will stop the child/teenager/criminal from going against my/our law in the future*!" What nonsense. Assumptions like this just alienate, and there is no evidence that compliance happens; except via fear used to control. If you want to live in a society which is dominated by fear, then live a life of punishment and retribution. If you want to live in a society which is dominated by love, model that by showing love, which means connecting to the person who has made the mistake, (by the way, sin means "missing the mark") and showing them a better way.

You see, UILE leads by example; no one is alone[70], we are all connected because we are all created from the same essence, all with the same shared spirit of love.

Our mission is to wisely align ourselves to compassion and love, for everyone. In order to do this we need to listen to the messages that come from UILE within us.

So, if we have an enemy, explore why. How can we align to the UILE within that person? We may hate their behavior, but still learn from it. Viktor Emil Frankl, M.D., Ph.D. was an Austrian neurologist and psychiatrist as well as a Holocaust survivor. Frankl was the founder of Logotherapy, which is a form of existential analysis founded upon the belief that it is the striving to find a love-based meaning in one's life that is the primary, most powerful motivating and driving force in humans.

> *"In some ways suffering ceases to be suffering at the moment it finds a meaning, such as the meaning of a sacrifice."*
> *Viktor Frankl, "Man's Search for Meaning"*

Through the depths of his experience in Kaufering, Auschwitz and Dachau, Frankl found a way to love, and gave mankind a gift of wisdom from his horror,

> *Love is the only way to grasp another human being in the innermost core of his personality. No one can become fully aware of the very essence of another human being unless he loves him.*
>
> *By his love he is enabled to see the essential traits and features in the beloved person; and even more, he sees that which is potential in him, which is not yet actualized but yet ought to be actualized.*
>
> *Furthermore, by his love, the loving person enables the beloved*

> *person to actualize these potentialities. By making him aware of what he can be and of what he should become, he makes these potentialities come true.*
>
> Viktor Frankl, *Man's Search for Meaning*

The poet Mary Oliver asks you "*Tell me, what is it you plan to do with your one wild and precious life?*" Don't waste the potential energy you have been given.

UILE is a concept which is a healthy archetype to describe the Tao, the Unknowable One; the Great Spirit. It does not carry the baggage of human based archetypes such as God being a white haired male human, and it carries both intimacy of our belonging within UILE, as well as the awe of UILE encompassing the entire time-based universe.

UILE is not a new concept of love. There have been those in all the major religious traditions who have held onto similar belief. They are known as the mystics; the word meaning "Inspiring a sense of mystery and wonder", and they come in all colors, countries and contexts.

Father Richard Rohr says,

> *Mystics always bring this message in some form: 'Do not be afraid.' They know that it is all okay and finally okay, too! They want to tell you so that you can stop fretting and fearing and enjoy divine union now. "Enjoy" is the operative word. Mystical experience allows you to enjoy your own life and to stop creating enemies and people to be afraid of and nations we have to punish and kill. When you are enjoying deep union, you won't need to create divisions, mistrust, and separation. Conspiracy theories and tabloid gossip hold little interest for you.*

The Islamic Sufi poet Hafez was born in Shiraz, Iran in the 14th century. Last year I was granted the gift of a beautifully illustrated copy of his work by my Iranian friend Ali. It is said that while working one day, Hafez encountered a being of surpassing beauty who identified himself as an angel, and from that encounter he became mystic; a pursuit of spiritual union with the divine. Energy comes in many forms, and the word angel actually means 'messenger', so it is no surprise that UILE provides messenger angels in every encounter with emotion, creativity and imagination.

I include a few lines from Hafez's beautiful poems to provide a feel for mystic joy and lack of fear. I hope you too resonate with them.

"Stay close to anything that makes you glad you are alive."
"Light will someday split you open"

"The earth has disappeared beneath my feet. It fled from all my ecstasy.
Now like a singing air creature I feel the rose keep opening."
"Fear is the cheapest room in the house.
I would like to see you living
In better conditions."

The energy of love comes to us in many ways, and it would be remiss if I didn't refer to the romantic and sexual love which is the form of love energy most sung and written about. I won't address this subject here other than to say that the energy of love can revolutionize lives, and certainly has with my life.

My wife Manu said to me this morning that there is significant energy in the alignment of the planets, and where there is more energy this affects human moods, sleep etc. Interesting that though I had always laughed at this in the past, now I am starting to see a long history of astrological thinking all of which concluded that major energy alignments can affect people. There are so many who believe in star signs etc., and who am I to poo-poo what I don't understand?

Love energy can revolutionize any part of life. If we are open to it, we can observe the potential energy of love in everything. That is the root of optimism. As the amazing lady Julian of Norwich[71], who was also a mystic, said in the 14th century, *"All shall be well, and all shall be well and all manner of things shall be well."* How is that for optimism, coming from a woman who lived in danger because of her teaching, in a time of great pessimism and plague? Julian's optimism is still felt today.

Optimism is another word for understanding UILE, because Intentional Love Energy shines as optimism. Intentional Love Energy is always available, because it is everywhere. Intentional Love Energy shines from inside you, your duty is to keep the lamp clean so you can see it within, and shine out to others. Give someone a compliment today. It costs nothing. Ask "Do you want that with a smile, and a hug?" Sure, I can risk doing that.

For those who like me, share an optimistic view of life, it is true, *"all you need is love"*.

> *See that I am God. See that I am in everything. See that I do everything. See that I have never stopped ordering my works, nor ever shall, eternally. See that I lead everything on to the conclusion I ordained for it before time began, by the same power, wisdom and love with which I made it. How can anything be amiss?*
>
> Lady Julian of Norwich

Summary

- Love Energy is your true character.
- Don't waste the potential energy you have.
- The pre-requisite to giving love is to accept love has meaning in everything, including ***your*** *wild and precious life.*
- You need not take anything personally, because *all will be well* in UILE.

- Allow your Love to shine out through optimism, joy and encouragement.

Chapter 12

Accepting Difference

To the people who love you, you are beautiful already. This is not because they're blind to your shortcomings but because they so clearly see your soul. Your shortcomings then dim by comparison. The people who care about you are willing to let you be imperfect and beautiful, too.
Victoria Moran, *Lit From Within: Tending Your Soul For Lifelong Beauty*

There is a common story told in North American tribal lore about a turkey living with eagles. It states that an egg is hatched by a turkey, but somehow the egg was really from an eagle, representing our connection to spirit. The problem is that this young bird is placed in a world of turkey thinking, and it will never soar if it thinks it is just a turkey.

The eagle grows up trying to be the best turkey it can be. It tries to feel comfortable with turkey thinking, but it is truly an eagle. We have both natures. There is a need for community feeding, and there is a need to fly high with spirit wings. When we see other eagles flying above us, we question, we long for the freedom and the destinations that become available to our higher selves.

Staying in the turkey realm is not wrong, but it is limiting. How does an eagle find its individuality and take the initiative to leave the flock and ascend?

Step 1 Recognizing Difference

It is impossible to fly unless you try.

But who will fly unless they believe they can? Who will act like an eagle unless they believe they are? Hence the first thing to do is to recognize effective patterns of behavior that are good models for yourself. If you recognize eagle wings exist on you, and you are seeing other eagles in your sky, perhaps you need to acknowledge the difference.

You may have been born into a family with rigid turkey beliefs. You may also have been told that you can only be a turkey, and that you should concentrate on the flock, that flying with eagles is dangerous to the flock, because eagles are the enemy! But deep within you there is an awareness that what you have been told, coached and coaxed is not the main game. You want more. You want to see the whole canvas?

It is not wrong to be different, but the demands of a group can be very limiting. What really matters to you? Do you want to be the eagle you recognize within?

Have you suppressed the call to abundance and bliss because you don't want to admit that you are capable, that you can be more?

Do you find that you have differences to others, and yet you feel a need to conform, despite the fact that it is limiting your bliss?

Each person on the planet and throughout history has uniqueness. You too! Identifying the difference between what your family/group/club sees you as, and your true nature, is essential to making change. Now you are ready to soar!

Step 2 Regulating Comparison

Unfortunately the first thing that typically happens when you look at how you may be different is to compare with others. That involves a value judgment on your difference. Value judgments need to be regulated.

If you compare and find yourself lacking, this requires an acceptance of who you are, much as you can fight an opponent in karate, or you can improve your own skills compared to yesterday. Observing higher performance as a goal is a good thing, but when it starts to bring you down, regulate the comparison, and revert to self-improvement.

On the other side, if you find yourself acting superior to another, this also requires regulation. While your performance in one instance may be superior to another, Love 101 teaches us that we should encourage, not put down. If we regulate comparison by encouraging, lifting and training those around us, we can all fly. The sky is limitless, there is room for all.

The golden rule could read, 'encourage others, as you would have them encourage you when you fall short."

Step 3 Attracting Other Eagles

By encouragement we can join in the creation of the highest order of things.

Knocking others down not only reduces the joy of high flying companions, it has a negative effect. You end up alone. Imagine the joy of flying and having a universe of beings wanting to join you, to reach new heights together!

What is important to your soul is attracted to you, as a result of a display of your life force energy. It is similar to the mating display of certain birds of Paradise. They cannot force a female to come to them. Their job is to present such an attractive display that the female will choose them. What a great example to us humans!

Professor Bruce Lipton explains how Noble gases form 'excimers' which are excited by the light, and in seeking bonding with another gas molecule they also generate light. The reason that laser lights operate is because triggered by light, excimers of Noble gas in proximity will emit their own powerful light. I find this a wonderful analogy of how we should live also.

Rather than wanting and lusting for what we do not have, we can display the wonder of who we actually are. Marianne Williamson says,

Our deepest fear is not that we are inadequate. Our deepest fear is that we are powerful beyond measure. It is our light, not our darkness that most frightens us. We ask ourselves, 'Who am I to be brilliant, gorgeous, talented, fabulous?' Actually, who are you not to be? You are a child of God.[72]

When we seek to be famous or attractive by what we accumulate, we miss this critical point that it is who we already are that needs to shine more than our worldly successes.

I am reminded of the touching story of the child with Down's syndrome who demonstrated what is really important.

Nine contestants, all physically or mentally disabled, assembled at a starting line for the 100-yard dash. They were all keen to run the race to the finish and win.

Towards the end, one little boy stumbled on the asphalt, tumbled over a couple of times, and began to cry. The contestants slowed down and looked back. Then they all stopped. Several went back to the fallen boy. One girl with Down's syndrome bent down and kissed him and said, *"This will make it better."*

Then some of them linked arms and walked together to the finish line. Everyone in the stadium stood, cheering, as the crowd was astonished as they observed what they themselves were unlikely to do: help a competitor.

So it is that if we choose to be who we truly are within, when we get in touch with the inner source of UILE and let it shine, we demonstrate our uniqueness and the resultant attractiveness. Everyone can do this, it is not about strength or intelligence, attractiveness is about inner acceptance and compassion. Think of the people who you know, respect and admire. Are they not the ones who shine with the joy of life, and who you just want to be near to share their enthusiasm? Do you not feel accepted in their presence?

So what is stopping each one of us from being attractive like that? The power of attraction that Marianne Williamson refers to is within, not external. It is the intention of Love.

Now on a planetary level if each of us can reflect the intention of acceptance rather than judgment, we will change the world. However it saddens me that even those who espouse religious belief often show dire non-acceptance and will even kill those who hold different beliefs. This is not love, and it demonstrates that their god is not UILE, but fear based. Behind this thinking of fear that somehow someone else's belief corrupts, is the paranoia that *they* who hold different views will get at *your* children and *corrupt* them, that *they* have some *control* over who you actually are. This is all rubbish. If you think like that, you are self-projecting; you are likely one of the *they*. Look to see if you are the one who in fear tries to use force to control your own children's beliefs, who seeks to control and influence others. Don't externalize and blame. Look in the mirror! You are not going to find joy in the practice of criticizing others, or copying their lives. Emulation and judgment are both insincere.

Yes, there are many initiatives towards multi-cultural dialog and acceptance, but it is you in particular who can change in this issue, which is as brutal and non-accommodating between scientists and religions as it is between those of different races and cultural habits. Can you accept everyone on the planet as equally valid as you? It is hard, especially when you think about someone who has harmed you recently, or who is attacking you. That is why when Jesus said, "love your enemies" the locals must have thought he had lost the plot.

Imagine there's no countries
It isn't hard to do
Nothing to kill or die for
And no religion too
Imagine all the people
Living life in peace…

You may say I'm a dreamer
But I'm not the only one
I hope someday you'll join us
And the world will be as one

Imagine no possessions
I wonder if you can
No need for greed or hunger
A brotherhood of man
Imagine all the people
Sharing all the world…[73]
John Lennon

Summary

- Difference is essential, and each individual is unique and wonderful.
- Comparison is only beneficial when it is used to encourage.
- Be the change yourself – don't compare, don't judge.

Chapter 13

Peace & Pain – Conflict with Negative-Ego

The first step to the knowledge of the wonder and mystery of life is the recognition of the monstrous nature of the earthly human realm as well as its glory, the realization that this is just how it is and that it cannot and will not be changed. Those who think they know how the universe could have been had they created it, without pain, without sorrow, without time, without death, are unfit for illumination.

Joseph Campbell

There is wisdom to be gained in experiencing any and all aspects of suffering, and particularly the emergence of embedded Negative-Ego internal negative thinking.

The blessing of abundant materialism in western society has led to less appreciation for the daily essentials, and resulted in a desire for more stuff which is not needed or valued. Compassion for suffering from lack of food or housing is distant and unconnected for most in western society. Similarly poor people must shake their heads in dismay when they read or watch wealthy people run amok with depression, self-abuse, suicide and addictions.

Buddha, Tolstoy, St. Francis, all have common stories.

They all came from wealthy families, endured war, discovered compassion for suffering, and then sought to understand about how to react to suffering. All ended their lives in peace, contentment, and without owning anything. Study and experience of suffering led them to want to discover how to reduce suffering.

Buddha concluded that suffering (dukkha) is caused by attachment and taught the eight-fold path as the way to cease suffering, Tolstoy thought that material desire creates false societal 'status quo' which perverts Christian love and joy, and St. Francis believed that suffering was overcome by constant spiritual awareness and admiration of the beauty, power and wisdom of creation. What is similar in the three different conclusions is a form of spiritual awareness. Awareness of a way to live authentically without being swamped by Negative-Ego is embodied in all their teachings.

Let's accept that we are in the dank, dark swamp of Negative-Ego right now. Who needs to be saved, to be pulled out? Everyone. Yes, everyone needs to be rescued from the way we view ourselves, from our own adherence to the stinking thinking of Negative-Ego. Salvation from suffering is getting to the point in life where nothing, attachment to material goods, political and organizational war or hate, nor pain or lack of money, have the ability to divert the soul's joy in celebrating right now the presence of love, beauty, joy and creativity with others.

As the 12-Step Program shows, we are all recovering addicts from that oozy black excrement of knocks, name-calling, rejection, and false information about who we are. We **don't have to be perfect** in order to enjoy bliss on this planet. Marianne Williamson says:

> *something amazing happens when we surrender and just love. We melt into another world, a realm of power already within us. The world softens when we soften. The world loves us when we choose to love the world.*

This does not mean that we don't suffer. M. Scott Peck noted, *"Life is difficult. Once (that) is accepted, the fact that life is difficult no longer matters."*[74] No longer matters? Who is he kidding? I just lost my job, my wife is threatening to leave me, and my kids are running rampant! OK. Those may be the facts. But do those life circumstances really affect who you are, what your essence is?

Consider your worst nightmare. Will it destroy the essential soul within you, or indeed could it be a way forward to the clarity that suffering is part of the human experience and can never destroy the Love inherent in UILE, in everything.

> *We who lived in concentration camps can remember the men who walked through the huts comforting others, giving away their last piece of bread. They may have been few in number, but they offer sufficient proof that everything can be taken from a man but one thing: the last of the human freedoms — to choose one's attitude in any given set of circumstances, to choose one's own way.*
> Viktor E. Frankl

You may well ask 'would I make such a difficult choice?', and there is no simple answer to this. Removing fear is perhaps the simplest key that fits the lock on the door to peace. Face the fear, face the loss such as that of Buddha's family, Tolstoy's wealth and reputation, St. Francis' health and death, and stare it in the face, sit with it till it becomes real; solid enough to fit into your personal keyhole.

How, you may ask, can befriending an emotion become a way to open up a door to your nirvana, heaven or just acceptance of yourself today?

The answer to that comes back to the reason you are unable to accept reality. You are not just a human body with a mind that has to solve this problem – that is Negative-Ego placing pressure on you to change what cannot be changed.

You are a specially formed spiritual being, an energy force of love, in the form right now of a human body. That is what UILE has coalesced into, and inside you **the capacity to live out a life of joy, compassion and meaning is not only possible, it is your destiny**. How long you take to absorb that reality is only an issue in that you are creating your own suffering right now if you live in the false illusion of the Negative-Ego.

> When we become willing to feel the pain, then we become capable of feeling the Joy. *The Joy of doing this healing is incredible!* Our job is to heal and enjoy! Our job is to be. We are here to be human beings, not human doings. Our job is to follow the joy to the Truth. Our job is to feel in the moment.[75]

Think of the worst possible thing that could happen to you. Think of loss such as of the one you love so much, to death, slavery, torture. There are many examples of people who chose, yes, *chose*, these options because they were not afraid of any of them. (Such choice is, incidentally, not my message.) The power of your spiritual being to utilize the connection to timeless love, and to right now be grateful of the gift you can give, be that a smile, a hug or a million dollars to a needy cause, that will center you on your true self, part of UILE.

OK, do you have your worst fear in your mind? Good. Now consider what power that fear has over you, given that you are a part of the Universal Intentional Love Energy; none. All will be well. You no longer need be afraid of your feelings, right, that you will not be able to cope. You no longer need be afraid that you will be left alone, unloved. You no longer need be afraid that others, in the same state as you, will reject you, shame you or hurt you.

But it is not easy to stay courageous. "What passes for morality or spirituality in the vast majority of peoples' lives is the way everybody they grew up with thinks. Some call it the crab bucket syndrome – you try to get out, but the other crabs just keep pulling you back in."[76]

Taking suffering 101 is a pre-requisite to compassion 101.

Being broken, joyful or fragile opens you up to love, to connection and to being attractive. Think of how you feel when you are in the presence of someone you know who has suffered as much or more than you. Do you find there are fewer barriers to being yourself with them? Jesus did not avoid the role of suffering and in his compassion through pain demonstrated this powerless nature of love. The simple fact is that power does not attract the heart, while a loving personality does.

Lynne Jacobs had a patient who was deeply ashamed of herself and considered herself to be inherently and irreparably defective. She also often believed that no one else in the world had the same problems that she had.

Lynne said "In the first few years I was so pained by her sense of shameful isolation, that I twice told her things about myself which were similar to problems she was describing. In both instances she became severely distressed, felt impinged on, and insisted that I never do that again. She said she needed me to be a "whole", not defective like herself."

This patient was looking at Lynne in a way that was unrealistic. By exposing her own frailties Lynne showed humanity, that no one is immune from the pain of life. It is common to want to present as a flawless being, without brokenness. Who would not want to be a diamond?

- A diamond is the hardest material in the world.
- It can easily score steel, glass, ceramics and other hard objects.
- However, it has another characteristic. It is easily shattered.

I remember reading a story by Wilbur Smith where a protagonist destroys millions of dollars of diamonds with a simple hammer and anvil. Seems such a waste, does it not? I am not surprised if the thought, "why didn't he give the diamonds away, or to me?" crosses your mind.

Yet our Negative-Egotistic nature pushes us to commonly perform the same wasteful destruction of each other. Behavior and words can act as a hammer on the inner value of the diamond within the recipient if action strikes against the anvil of negative interpretation.

Experience which puts down or diminishes the higher self, that part of self that is connected to the eternal, can also be a hammer that smashes the diamond within.

Here is a poem I wrote in 2004:

Shattered

My son's death
smashed into me like a hammer
into a sheet of ice.
I exploded into a million pieces,
some sharp shards cutting
those around me,
while other fragments,
warmed by empathy,
melt into tears.

Cold and broken
I will be.
Till hope can slowly
cover me.

The amazing aspect about our inner selves is that we can be reconstructed by hope, and love, and regain the ability to shine. Richard Bach wrote in his book *Illusions* *"The mark of your ignorance is the depth of your belief in injustice and tragedy. What a caterpillar calls the end of the world the master calls a butterfly."*

Having been given the beauty of dreams that have re-introduced my lost son as a joyful butterfly of light with UILE, eight years later I was able to write this poem.

Find the Beauty

Hope is not gone:
It resides in beauty, which adorns every path

if you look for it.
Find the beauty in a plant squeezing its way up through the city concrete.
Find the beauty in the smile of a child who has been encouraged by kindness.
Find the beauty in the evening stars who have always been sentinels of ordered light.
Be beautiful yourself by embracing compassion, love and peace.
Search, and you will always find, a rock, a pool, a sparkling eye, a transient glimpse of life in the wild.

Sometimes, just sometimes, beauty will flood your senses
And you at those times will know beauty is an infinite wisdom from UILE that flows into us as a gift.
At times when empty, look inside to find the source roadmap of where beauty is to be found.
The map shows life in abundance, a joy and peace beyond understanding, an intense inner knowing that there is more.
Find the beauty within,
for the roads that open from that soul-intersection are many,
each path will contain more flowers, scenes, and creative art
to enjoy with the laughter of friends along the way,
than you ever thought possible!
Hope is not gone:
It resides in beauty.
And beauty is eternal and part of the infinite spirit.
Philosofree

The beauty and value of a diamond is within you, and your light can shine again even after being shattered, or covered with the excrement from others.

Mary Oliver said it well; *"Someone I loved once gave me a box full of darkness. It took me years to understand that this too, was a gift."* Remember the chapter above on space? Recall that energy exists in the space, that light actually travels in the blackness of the void, but it needs to interact to be seen. So it is with our inner darkness. The light is there all the time; it is the energy of UILE in the form of light, present but needing a place to shine. You are that place. Shine on!

Summary

- Pain, Sorrow and Grief are the seeds of our later joy.
- In darkness we find the source of light.
- Hope is the first and necessary precursor to inner growth and optimism.

Chapter 14

Living in Balance

Who isn't plagued most of a lifetime by this duality of life? Masculine and feminine voices within, duty or desire, good or evil, this choice or that choice, follow my heart or follow my mind – we can go on forever reciting the pairs of opposites that express the yin and yang of life.
Robert A Johnson

How to stay balanced on a tight rope? Try a long pole that extends from one extreme to the other. As you find yourself leaning one way, lean the other. Or is there a Zen-like question we should be asking ourselves? Maybe we should be leaning **inwards**.

Let me present a classic challenge to your thinking. For example, bring into your mind the first thing you think of when you recall a 'spoilt child.' Did you think negatively at the concept? Now consider someone that you know that you might have put that label on, it could be a child or an adult, and consider what is behind the judgment in the phrase. What does it mean, this spoilt or spoiled-ness? It means the character or nature of someone is damaged by "excessive, self-centered, and immature behavior". From early in our lives we are challenged to consider certain behaviors as wrong. However right and wrong infers good and bad, so it is more useful to consider unbalanced which means consequences. Let's look as some examples:

- An apple left in the heat rots. If it is left in the snow, it freezes and loses its firmness when thawed. In both cases we say the apple is 'spoiled.'

- A person learning to ride a pushbike will lean one way or the other, and if they go too far, they will fall, and suffer the consequences.
- Pampering a child means that they don't get to experience their own independence, their own choices and the realities of life. On the other hand insufficient attention and pampering with affection, as was discovered with the orphans of Romania, will result in their demise.
- If we seek release when we suffer pain instead of learning from the experience,then the pain moves from a gift to become something we avoid. Conversely if pain is sought rather than observed, as in hypochondria, its purpose is corrupted.

As in all the above cases, moving to an extreme on the spectrum of choice results in adverse consequences. Balance is at the heart of your health. Encourage those around you to achieve balance and you will bond with that person.

A classic example of balance is in how you spend your time. "All work and no play makes Jack a dull boy" was an old saying. But what is play? Is it sitting in front of someone else's life or dreams, watching a movie, TV, or computer screen? I don't think so, while that may be rest, it may also just be wasting your precious lifetime. But play is a different thing entirely because it exercises imagination. Think of play as wrestling with a child, building a tree house, mud fights etc. It opens you to awareness and joy at the same time. Play is really interaction with others where there is shared joy in the activity.

I am not denying that there can be a sense of satisfaction from playing a computer game or watching a movie. But it is another form of dulling the senses, of running away from who you are into someone else's reality. I see entertainment like any addictive behavior that leads away from bliss. The classic example is 'reality TV' which is at best voyeurism, yet you could be living an even more meaningful life where you are right now! Sams and Carson in the book *Medicine Cards* write: "*Anything less than the doing of that which gives you the most joy is denial.*"

What are you looking for? Are you looking to be famous, while you ignore the ones around you who want you to shine for *them*? Seriously, does anyone get joy from addictive things that deep inside lead to self-diminishment? Why choose such repetitive behavior instead of returning to the freedom you always wanted, where you will get joy and happiness, to the higher self you really are?

Just like you don't accidentally eat anything, you don't accidentally choose your work or hobbies or play or indulgences. But you may have convinced yourself that you didn't have a choice, that there 'wasn't anything else to do' or that 'I couldn't bear sitting and thinking of my situation of pain, loss, rejection or whatever, and so I had to eat, pop a pill, play a game, watch a movie etc.'

Boredom

Consider this simple question.

If you continued to do an activity exclusively, what would be the effect? Would your higher-self approve of it? If repetition is just filling in your hours because you are bored with life, have a good look at the gap between your dreams and your life. You cannot be bored when you are in touch with your true self. Every true self moment is an opportunity or an inspiration. As the Danish existentialist philosopher Soren Kierkegaard so precisely said, "*Boredom is the root of all evil – the despairing refusal to be oneself.*"

If you are doing what you love, your true calling, and inspired and joyful doing it, then you can do it with balance and joy, allowing time for when your body calls for rest, time to have fun, to enjoy food, friendship and to help others.

Often we continue to move like pendulums, swinging from

one extreme to another, or worse still, lose energy and sit without moving, afraid to investigate life at either extreme because of what we have been told. *"Children are to be seen but not heard."* What rubbish. We learn from experience. From the falling down, grasping a moment of truth at the bottom of the arc, then up the other side till we stall. Down, up, down, up, in a sort of hamster wheel of trying to be balanced. We struggle to understand the extremes so we can know where the sweet spot is.

The truth is that only love can provide the sense of gravity we need, to calibrate where our center should be. Our center of gravity is actually UILE, the love energy that will pull us to our center, where balance provides meaning. So we need to listen to our own energy, and the pull it exerts on us will lead us to our true 'home' on the balance scale. Nothing else will; book knowledge won't, other people can't, experience is relative depending on where we are on the swing, and we cannot rely on tradition in a world of change. We are called to look inside.

> *"As surely as there is a voyage away, there is a journey home."*
> Jack Kornfield, *After the Ecstasy, the Laundry*

I wish to redefine some words, within the paradigm that Universal Love is the intention of all existence, and that all is held softly within that Love.

Humbleness

Humbleness, the concept of being humble, will be better defined as 'not seeing yourself, or any part of creation, as being worth less than yourself.' How can your arm be less important than your eye? Sure it has a different function, for example the eye can't lift things as well as an arm, but the body needs both. So the body of all creation similarly needs each and every aspect to be whole. No being is worth less than you, and should be respected accordingly. Even the mother earth deserves such respect, for just as we likely have atoms in us from people who are dead and decomposed back into earth, so she holds us all in the end, and is herself just a small part of UILE. We will all return to the same earth, and our soul will continue to be energy outside of time, where I believe we will review our own behaviors while in time, as is reported by many who have had near-death experiences.

Balance juggles both your smallness and insignificance along with your one-ness with the magnificent UILE. As Jack Kornfield said, "*Wisdom says we are nothing. Love says we are everything. Between these two our life flows.*"

The mirror concept to being humble is self-love or confidence. This is better defined as '*always seeing yourself as of value and worth, never believing that you are loved less than another.*' Self-love is an absolutely crucial pre-requisite to humbleness, as it defines within your soul that you are important, and worthy, and hence have a firm anchor to hold that same principle for others.

Ownership

The concept of ownership can also then be seen to require reconsideration.

Given that we are all part of the same entity, how can we own anything? Sure we can hold or use something, a dollar, a car, a house, but it is only temporary. Which part of us owns that thing, if we are all one? We should respect it, for sure, as if it were someone else's and we have it on loan, and that applies to how we handle money, material goods, the environment, and ***especially*** the bodies of other people.

Most men, for example, can relate to looking at an attractive woman and having the negative-ego reaction "I want that woman in my harem", even though our conscious mind identifies this as primal animal instinct, and if we are already in a relationship we recognize the thought is illogical (harems are not possible) and antisocial (it diminishes the woman by basing a decision on hormones rather than character, and prioritizes looks above commitment).

Any action we take which disrespects the body of another or places them as less than us, is wrong. That includes slavery, prostitution, excess work demands, or put down comments. This theme is the prime driver behind the first book of my *Bion & Freya* fiction trilogy. Such judgmental disrespect invokes a cosmic law that calls for punishment of the action, because both the deed and the punishment are consequences that affect us all. That is the true meaning of karma, not that it will come back to bite us individually, but that right now it is biting the cosmic whole, of which you are part.

Richard Rohr's phrase "stinking thinking" is about the universal addiction to external sources to achieve wholeness. It stinks because when you look outside your soul, towards time-based solutions, you are forced to compete. However, if everyone was calmly satisfied with their life, they could spend their days creating and giving in joy, rather than feel an obligation to fill the gaping pit of need.

Discerning beauty, identifying things to be grateful for, these are always soul food. Looking to food, drugs, entertainment, etc., as pleasures is not going to satisfy. Thinking about collecting money and resources which will later purchase these time-based pleasures is even further away from reality.

Pleasure

True pleasure is in working together right now to build or create something. That something *created* may be as simple as a hug, and joy comes from the giving of it.

Soren Kierkegaard says it better than I can; *"The highest and most beautiful things in life are not to be heard about, nor read about, nor seen but, if one will, are to be lived."*

Think of your own experience in those times when you happily created something, say a gift of art, for someone else.

Think quietly about those times, and see if there is not a deep sense of "who you are" that comes through that. Do you think that deep sense of authenticity can be achieved by slaving at work to get money to purchase a life of 'luxury' where you 'don't have to work'? I ask that I be given the blessing of being able to contribute my time in meaningful work to the day I die, which is what I call heaven. Retirement to some artificial beach contemplating my navel over an endless procession of cocktails holds no attraction to the sparkling colors of creating a meal for well-loved friends and then singing together in happiness for the day.

> *For the first time in my life I saw the truth as it is set into song by so many poets, proclaimed as the final wisdom by so many thinkers. The truth – that Love is the ultimate and highest goal to which man can aspire. Then I grasped the meaning of the greatest secret that human poetry and human thought and belief have to impart: The salvation of man is through love and in love.*
> Viktor Frankl, *Man's Search for Meaning*

Awareness

When I sit with any creation of love, such as art, scripture, or nature itself, if I am open to it, something may stand out to me. This is the Lectio Divina, a long-standing tradition of being aware of what is in wisdom scriptures, also applicable to every aspect of love's presence. It is an ancient way to "hear" with all five senses, and thus be ready to attend to the emotional reaction that is happening within you. Each person will be informed by their own soul, if there is an attitude of being ready for inspiration. What is the source saying to us? Traditionally there are four steps.

1 observe/absorb,
2 meditate about it, in silence,
3 allow the energy to flow between UILE and your soul, and

4 contemplate the message of love that is carried.

Awareness is recognizing UILE in all life, in all spirit and in all creation. By respecting the inner voice with a consistent method or practice each day, you are exercising your soul. A simple way of doing this is to look for, and sit with, something you can learn and/or be grateful for every day.

Summary

- Life is a balancing act, requiring us to stay alert to the present moment.
- Balance is only meaningful when we choose Love as the center of gravity.
- You do not need external approval to be what you truly are already; a personality of Intentional Love Energy, part of UILE.
- Love is the highest goal, and it is woven deeply into our deepest passions.
- Practice daily awareness, attend to what your soul interprets from each reality you face.

Chapter 15

Authenticity

God does not like to be worshipped by an ignorant man who imitates someone else
Khalil Gibran, from *Khalil the Heretic*

Be yourself! It sounds so logical and so easy, doesn't it!

However, we have already looked at how the great mass of our being is wrapped in the subconscious, and if we spend our lifetime mining this wealth we can reach a point where we are truly who we are, truly authentic.

David Aaron says that, "*as babies we knew the truth but then we lost it. We are in recovery!*" Our search within is where we find wholeness. But how do we know if we have reached awareness, or are becoming authentic?

China's Tao Te Ching suggests:

Humans must achieve the ultimate void and maintain calmness with sincerity in order to observe the growth and flourishing of all beings.
It is in this way that one can understand the law of nature.
All things and beings will eventually return to the original source.
This is called "peace."
"Peace" means returning to one's original nature.

What is our original nature? At the risk of appearing repetitive, our original, and still our only *true* nature, is that we are one with all. In recognizing the one-ness with UILE, with all energy, the Force, God, the Great Spirit, or whatever Unnameable concept you have, one becomes free from the weird Negative-Ego accusation that you are bad, destined for punishment, or worse that you will spend eternity in survival guilt! UILE cannot be Love and yet have fear as an outcome. Love wins in the end, because at the end of time there is only the energy of Love remaining. That is what we know about this earth and matter. Eons may seem a long time, but time ceases to exist once the matter returns to its source, energy.

We dance for laughter, we dance for tears,
we dance for madness, we dance for fears,
we dance for hopes, we dance for screams,
we are the dancers, we create the dreams.
Albert Einstein

So it is that to live authentically we must live with passionate energy, part of all UILE, and in and with Love. From that point we then are called to abundance in every moment of time available to us. I wrote this for a dear friend, but it is applicable for you too:

Get back on your horse,
and ride.

Not someone else's horse,
not a wooden horse,
not your child's
or your spouse's horse,
but ***your*** *horse,*

the one you have always had.

The horse that can run free,
and laugh,
and run to wild horizons,
and does not accept corrals and walls,

that understands only opening gates
and new meadows
and the wind in the mane.

Ride free
Now.
Each second at a time.

(maybe building up speed
to one minute at a time.)

Get back on your horse,
and ride

bareback!
Philosofree

Elements of Authenticity

We cannot be authentic if we lack the elements of authenticity:

- An accurate view of self, which requires optimal utilization of feedback from others.
- A helicopter view of self-awareness, and an un-biased self-examination.
- Reflective judgment, that differentiates between the behavior and the worth of a person – e.g. it is necessary to assess one's actions and critique them, but not with any associated guilt or shame. (More about that in chapter 20!)
- Responsibility and integrity with a thought-through moral and ethical framework.
- Genuineness and humility which shows through empathy for other people.

In order to achieve this, we need to act:

1 Honestly – Value truth, be proud of having necessary internal arguments between moral alternatives to identify the truth within yourself.
2 Clearly and concisely, communicating only when the truth needs to be told.
3 Non-judgmentally – Speak about what you are experiencing, not blaming.
4 In the moment – be relevant and timely, supporting what your higher self believes.

Summary

- Be yourself, not the puppet of someone else's Negative-Ego.
- Your personality is unique – don't hide it, let it 'roar'.
- To act authentically you will act in Love! This means don't just do something, sit there!
- Humans all have a heart of love, our own lightness of spirit comes when we can ignore the Negative-Ego behaviors that hide the light.[77]
- Apply the elements or guidelines for assessing authenticity.

Section Four – Outside of Time

In Section One, time is shown to be linked to existence as we know it in a human body. Now it is time to look at reality, authenticity, death, resurrection and dream voices that transcend time.

Chapter 16

The Mandala Turns

Between the people of eternity and the people of the earth there is a constant communication, and all comply with the will of that unseen power
Kahlil Gibran[78]

Consider the concept of reincarnation. Most people, including most Christians[79], believe in reincarnation! Does that surprise you? Reincarnation or 'being recreated after death into flesh (carnal) form again' has two main interpretations. The first is a new incarnation or embodiment in human flesh, called resurrection.

You may not have studied the Jewish faith, and its rich heritage, but most western people would know that Christianity, Islam and the Jewish religions are all based on Abrahamic background, in other words they all arose from a Jewish background and revere Old Testament books in common.

All the Abrahamic religions believe that the dead and living will be reborn.[80] Many Christians and Jews believe that a physically new Jerusalem will be created where humans will be reinstituted into their human form.

Of course a further extension of reincarnation is where you have another life after dying, with your soul being born into another human body at a later time. If you too think this is possible, you are not alone. Lisa Miller, the religion editor for *Newsweek* wrote the book *Heaven: Our Enduring Fascination with the Afterlife,* in which she quotes indicators that a quarter of Americans now believe in this sort of reincarnation. Rev. Brian Weiss has a series of internationally popular books teaching people how to experience past life regression, dipping into the experiences of previous lives.

If you do not agree with reincarnation, you may be one of many who see it as a way of avoiding 'Judgment Day', which is viewed as an assessment of a person's worthiness to enter God's presence for eternity. Why would the Universe of Love reject any of the life it created? This is indeed life-sapping judgment, the very thing that Jesus preached against. You would be right though; to believe in reincarnation typically is at odds with the concept of "going to hell (punishment) for eternity". To be punished in physical forms, as some believe, is to believe you will have a body after death.

Reincarnation is not a new concept or belief; there are many interesting, ancient, concepts about reincarnation worth considering even if you don't believe in them.

Indian belief as early as 600 BCE has recorded instances of clear belief in reincarnation. The Upanishads refer to the belief.

Plato quotes Socrates as saying in 400 BCE: *"I am confident that there truly is such a thing as living again, and that the living spring from the dead."* There was certainly a Greek thread of reincarnation belief, such as the Orphic religion. In fact Plato believed that we gradually move closer and closer to God through reincarnation as well as in our individual lives. He also thought our ethical goal in life was to come closer to the spiritual world, to liberate ourselves from matter, time, and space, and to become more real in this deeper sense. Plato's goal was, in other words, self-realization.

The mystical beliefs of Jewish faith, resident in the Kabbalah's "Book of Reincarnation", hold that there are four options to life after death. These are:

1 A direct pass to heaven.
2 A temporary holdup on the way for up to 12 months (though if you are outside time I don't understand how you would measure a year) which is very similar to the

Catholic purgatory, and the likely source of this belief.

3 Reincarnation because you haven't finished the goal or purpose you were sent here for.
4 The dead soul is a ghost so attached to materialist things that the soul can't bear to leave, so it is in limbo till it chooses to leave its attachment and try for re-entry. This incidentally is as close to hell as it gets.

In Kabbalistic belief, once again, someone is assessing life against some value or goal, except that it looks like the assessor is oneself, which is interesting. This is consistent with near-death experiences which are well documented and commonly include an analytical life review.

What about other Jewish belief? Jesus of course was a Jew, and may have prayed this ancient prayer of the Jews which is still in use today:

> Master of the Universe, I hereby forgive anyone who has angered me, or vexed me or sinned against me, either physically or financially against my honor or anything else that is mine, whether accidentally or intentionally, inadvertently or deliberately, by speech or by deed, **in this incarnation or any other**.

Bearing in mind that the Jewish Torah (The Old Testament of the Bible) was written after the escape from Egypt, and the Egyptian emphasis on the afterlife, it is surprising that the afterlife is not really addressed in the Torah. Rabbi Telushkin points out that Egyptian society was obsessed with life after death. Their holiest text was called "The Book of the Dead," and both mummification and tombs like the pyramids were meant to prepare a person for existence in the afterlife.

These examples show the Abrahamic traditions as well as the Eastern religions incorporated reincarnation belief in their background. Western civilization has suppressed discussion on reincarnation. What is the motivation for such suppression? The motivation is primarily about theology. If you believe that reincarnation allows a further spiritual growth, it is illogical to threaten hell and damnation after a specific death, which is the prime theological control weapon used in all Abrahamic religious structures over the past two millennia.

But surely Christians cannot believe in reincarnation into another person? Would that not mean that Christ's message was false? I invite you to consider that it is through the grace of Love that we are saved, not from an external place of hell and damnation, but saved instead from the darkness of Negative-Ego, of our own making. Therefore it is the eternal soul, the energy-spirit, which experiences eternal one-ness, and that soul can be growing in awareness across multiple incarnations. Christians believe that Jesus will return in renewed body, why should it be strange for others to also?

I believe that punishment was not consistent with the acceptance and love Jesus showered on everyone that he encountered, irrespective of whatever faults, reputation or theology practiced. Jesus' life ended with him telling the dying thief on the cross, *"Today you will be with me in paradise"*. That could have been any human.

Could it be that punishment after death was not taught by Jesus? Could it be that afterlife punishment was added to Jesus' words by the church over time? There is good reason to consider this.

Consider these words of Jesus to the church leaders of his time.

Jesus said,

> *Yes, and I tell you that crooks and whores are going to precede you into God's kingdom. John (the Baptist) came to you showing you the right road. You turned up your noses at him, but the crooks and*

whores believed him. Even when you saw their changed lives, you didn't care enough to change and believe him.
Matt 21:31, 32

Ancient Christian texts unearthed in 1945 display compelling similarities between Gnostic conceptions of life and death and modern near-death experiences. The Gnostics were a strong 'heresy' which was persecuted by the church power-base during the first centuries after Jesus' death.

One important Christian Gnostic teaching was the "Logos" which in Greek is translated as "the image of the Word." It is an important concept found in the gospel of John (which is a key book of the New Testament of the Bible):

"In the beginning was the Word (Logos), and the Word was with God, and the Word was God." (John 1:1)

Logos is the part of God that acts in the world. It is the perfect unity of the human and the divine. This is affirmed by John later in his book when he wrote that *"the Word was made flesh and dwelt among us."* Is it reasonable to translate this 'Word' as UILE energy? John had no other easy way to describe the concepts that I outline in this book. Word in the Greek, can be interpreted as 'command' or 'intent made known'. I believe John was talking about UILE.

When John stated that Jesus is the Logos, he is stating that Jesus became the Logos, the Christ. The Logos is the divine "spark" of God within humans that needs to awaken. Everyone has the "image of the Word (Logos)" within them and it is for this reason that Genesis describes humanity as created *"in the image and likeness of God."*

The Logos is the divine Spirit in humanity. By using the Christian Gnostics' idea of the Logos, John is not only affirming the pre-existence and divinity of Jesus, but he is affirming that all people created in the "image of the Word" as Jesus was pre-existed in spirit before being born. In other words, every human is an incarnation of the Logos and every human has the potential of becoming like Jesus, a manifestation of the human-divine unity. Gnostics therefore believe that every human can be a "Christ" and because of this, every soul will eventually be drawn back to God. This was a common belief after Jesus died. Many thousands were persecuted and killed by the church for this belief, and this is well recorded in history.

You may have read *The Da Vinci Code*, Dan Brown's book that talked about early texts that showed new ways of seeing Jesus, and the role of women in the church? He was talking about the Gospel of Thomas, which has been reliably dated as the earliest of the Christian writings still available. It is also possibly linked with the "Q Source" which is the now lost earlier writings that recorded fragments of what Jesus said, and from which the other gospel writers drew their content.

The overriding concern of the Gospel of Thomas is *to find the light within*, in order to be a light unto the world. (See for example, Sayings 24, 26.)

The following quote from the Gospel of Thomas can also be interpreted as Jesus teaching reincarnation to his disciples:

> *When you see your likeness, you are happy. But when you see your images that came into being before and that neither die nor become visible, how much you will bear!*
> *(Gospel of Thomas, saying 84)*

Do these examples prove anything? No. However, by opening your mind to the possibilities, it can help you to battle negative perceptions laid down like layers of rock over the centuries, constructs of thought that hold that you are essentially bad, and in need of external action in order to be your true self. This is the voice of defeatist control, used by religion and institutions to build reliance and thought slavery. The spirit of Love is within you.

Reincarnation is consistent with ongoing growth, lack of fear of death, and a loving call for compassion to never give up on anyone. No wonder many institutions argue against it, when it opens the door for each individual to be free to choose their own path to understanding and wisdom.

Searching within for truth, and allowing yourself the freedom to consider that this may be one of multiple lives you have led, is a path I have found interesting and rewarding. You may have a struggle with Negative-Ego if you do it is because coming back into another body implies that acceptance and love continue forever, and this of course is a very positive and healthy stance, which threatens your Negative-Ego.

Summary

- The wheel of life turns inexorably, there is no reason why this is your soul's only life.
- People have believed in reincarnation for millennia, it is not a new or radical belief, but there is no proof of afterlife resurrection or reincarnation.
- Reincarnation belief implies no one will be damned or cut off from the Universal Spirit.
- Your Negative-Ego may resist the implicit acceptance and love within reincarnation.

Chapter 17

Death is Not Something to Fear

To live is nothing more than to come here to die, to be what we were before being born, but with apprenticeship, experience, knowledge of cause, and perhaps with will.
Juan Ramón Jiménez

Negative-Ego would have you believe that the center of the universe is – you!

The cunning thing about this thought is that in a sense it is true. Your individual world of experience is unique and totally about you. It is so easy to think that everyone around you should be aware of you, pay attention to you, as you are unique. As a baby this was indeed your experience!

Growing up, everyone reaches the same dilemma. Who is going to do the giving? Not everyone can be at the center of society. Observation of the world as negative, belief that everything is bad, and getting worse, is in fact based on insufficient skills to battle the Negative-Ego. And one of the best weapons Negative-Ego has in its armory is "the scythe of death". *'Life is hard and bad, and then you die!'*

What is it that allows fear about death to be so prevalent? Not everyone is afraid of death. Those who, like me, believe in Love and life in the present moment don't fear death. This also applies to those who believe their lives will continue to reincarnate until merging back into the Spirit of Love.

Place my soul in a coffin

Place my soul in
A coffin

Made from my own wood,
(not some 'must' or 'should')
Sprouted from a seed
(miracle indeed)
that is planted
(where it is needed)
in my heart
(broken apart)
when it comes to know
(as Love shows)
It won't die
(nor will the real I)
But sink into earth
(the place of rebirth)
Love germinated.
(abundance is freed)
Then I'll grow
roots and know,
that my limbs will extend
(with every new friend)
into infinite skies.
(of possibilities)
When I am lopped
(we learn from each chop)
The planks that are made
(the part that I gave)
will make my own coffin.
(for all fear within)
So I will joyfully leave
(and continue to give)
Experience behind
(as I choose to shine)
And return to the whole
(the infinite goal)

Where I came from;
(and will always belong)
Love's undying song.
Philosofree

My advice is to face Negative-Ego within you. You don't have to suffer the emotion of fear, you can befriend it, hear what it is telling you.

Beliefs of negativity and punishment are learned, they are not your true nature. Fear is telling you that negativity *is* your true nature. It's your call. Which alternative is true to you?

If you want to release fear, jump into its darkness. You will find you are not dashed to pieces or scared witless. As you face the fear, it shows you its message. Fear has a message that sounds implausible. Fear's message, like the message of pain, is one that cries for attention to restore health. Listen to it.

Fear impolitely says, "Pay attention to me, please! I, your fear, want you to know that Love, peace, bliss and joy can be rediscovered. My job is to stop you from taking these already existing emotions of your true being for granted. Spend time in quiet. Spend time playing forward the Love you discover is already in you!"

However, Negative-Ego argues that the fear associated with death is because you deserve punishment, hell and damnation. That is a power influenced belief, projected and taught by those who wish to control. Have a think about the motives of those who may have taught such negatives. Was the motive fear or love?

John Lennon asked us to imagine there is no hell, and I wonder if that is an issue for you? If you do believe in a place of punishment and torment, what does that say about the universe and the threat to your role in eternity?

Can you allow yourself the freedom to let punishment go? Judging, (which is discussed in chapter 16) is the pre-requisite of punishment. This concept that 'breaking the law' should result in punishment has no merit in fact. Is the law really broken if someone disobeys? No.

Consider the results of punishment. On a micro scale, do you really feel comfortable with putting people in prison for their mistakes or wrongdoings? Have you thought about how you would feel if you were judged guilty for a crime and sent to prison? Does punishment help anyone? I think everyone can agree that the few people who are genuinely psychopathically dangerous should be kept isolated in hospital prison for their and others' sakes. But apart from that, where is the benefit? It costs huge amounts of money, the track record of remediation is dreadful, and on release the ex-prisoner's prospects are bleak.

What about the death penalty? That is another 'punishment'. Do we have the right to kill another because we assess their crime punishable by death? On a higher scale, look at the punishment meted out on the German nation after the loss of World War One. Did that help anyone? It is almost certainly the main motivator for World War Two.

It is a vexed subject, but the old Jewish law of 'a tooth for a tooth' is one of fear, not love, and causes more pain. If we look at the very top level of punishment, it is based on the same premises:

A There is an external God or Gods (most history shows the spirit within, not without).

B God(s) think of justice in a human sense (though Jesus was against judgment).

C Everyone is subject to punishment for mistakes (though this is how we learn).

D The ultimate punishment is remaining in human form and being tortured in hell (yet when we die international experience of near-death is of love coming in a white channel and feeling peace).

This is human thinking, promulgated by those who wish to control other people into doing what they want from fear. You can now take a deep breath and let that go. That is what Universal Love would have you do.

Another fear is that of loss. Loss is another issue of space. (Recall Chapter 3?)

We all want belonging, but who is the belonging to be with?

At a recent gathering a friend was in tears talking about the death of the person she worked closely with. She missed him, and during discussion we identified it was her loss that was the hardest part. So I told her about the dream I had of my son after he had died, coming back all smiles and hugging me. After I explained that she can still listen for his spirit, that he will still hear her inner loss, she calmed down and later said that her loss was diminished, just by sitting with it, and taking the positive dream into her being.

Waiting for the star.
Evening.
A time of pondering the past day.
Darkness slowly sweeping its hand across the harsh realities
and from the folds of mother night
the peace of rest is unwrapped;
waiting for the star
that will flash into our lives
with the brightness
of eternal space.
Philosofree

This poem is talking about death, the presence of death as rest, as refreshment, with the sparkling eyes of the poet unchanging as the evening comes.

Think about your own freedom. Can you be free to choose if you are fearful? What leads us to fear of death? Is it a bogeyman created by someone to get you to do what they want? If you think so, then open your heart to love, love the inner presence of the energy of love within. You cannot respect that implicit wonder of universal love if you do not see it within yourself.

Death is not negative. It is the Return to Love. [81]

Summary

- The fear of death is that life ends, in suffering, punishment or nothingness.
- Life is good when it is lived authentically in the space of the present moment.
- Time is absorbed back into a universal energy that includes us, even after death.
- You are a spiritual being in a physical body.

Chapter 18

Dream Stories

The Gods, as the Greeks conceived them, were forces that interacted with individual human lives. These forces were present in every life, yet were universal, timeless, and lived outside the limits of a particular life or time. 'The Gods' could as well as been described as 'fields of energy' acting on the human race. Yet their images presented integrated personalities that are similar to the persons in our dreams who carry an aura of great power.
Robert A Johnson; *Inner Work*

Saint John of the cross (1542-1591) told the following story:

Once upon a time there was a man who was a good man, who had a family he loved and cared for. He worked hard to supply his family with the things they needed, but he was unable to earn sufficient to meet their needs. He started to worry about them, and it was his practice to pray for advice at a lovely little chapel in his village.

On one occasion while praying an angel appeared and said "Follow me", so the man tracked after the angel who led him deep into an ancient forest. The angel looked at the man with meaning, and said "dig here" and the man was naturally a bit concerned and hesitant. The angel said "now!" and the man started to dig with his bare hands. He found the going tough and nothing was showing up, but experienced the strength of his youth return, so while the angel stood over him with resolve, he continued to dig deeper and deeper.

Once he was as far down as he could go without falling into the hole he had dug, his fingers struck something hard in the soft earth. Excitedly the man uncovered a lost treasure which changed his fear to joy, and he was never the same again. He turned to the angel who said "dig here" with a shining face, and the angel looked at him kindly and said "in your soul, in your soul you dug".

St. John's moral for this story was that finding the beauty in our soul gives us a tremendous freedom from worry.

We may wonder how to go about digging deep in the soul. However, the messages from the history of mystery are clear. Dreams are a great tool to dig with.

Consider the story of the dream of Nebuchadnezzar, who was king of Babylon about 600 BC. It was a disturbing dream. So, the king of what was the greatest empire in history to that date demanded that his wise men both tell him what he had dreamed and what it meant! Naturally they couldn't, so Nebuchadnezzar summarily ordered the execution of them all. Probably a tad dictatorial, but it had the effect he wanted. The wise men were beside themselves.

At that time some of the Jewish captives lived in Babylon, one of them was called Daniel. His story is told in the Old Testament of the Bible in the Book of Daniel. In Daniel 2:27 it says Daniel replied, "No wise man, astrologer, magician, or wizard can tell the king such things, but there is a God within who reveals secrets, and he has told you in your dream what will happen in the future."

Then Daniel went on to describe the dream and what it meant. Pretty impressive! Nebuchadnezzar thought so too, gave him many gifts, and promoted the Jewish captive to chief magistrate in the king's court. It is a classic story about dreams and the connection to a mystery which is beyond any explanation known. The story continues with Nebuchadnezzar losing his sanity and his rule over the then known world. However, most remarkably, Nebuchadnezzar came through his years of inner turmoil, and returned to become even more a true emperor of the world. What miracles can occur when we pay attention to our inner messages?

In the 21st century the miracles still continue, the soul is still being mined for the presence of treasures. That is not just the domain of psychologists and doctors. Each one of us can learn about ourselves more.

Last night I had a conversation with a friend who said she didn't dream at all. I asked her to go to bed with two intentions, one to be welcoming to any dream messages and secondly to write down any small snippets of dream that can be remembered when she woke. Her reaction was interesting. "Oh I had that sort of tiny occurrence last night, but I didn't think it was a dream, just a sort of funny thought while I was sleeping". Yep, this woman who didn't dream was in fact becoming aware. We may all dream, but we may not all pay attention or recall, and many of us don't consider dreams as valuable. They are!

There are many ways to interpret dreams; many approaches. Many ways of using dreams as a means of telling someone what to do; but your dreams are for you alone, and they need to have your input to unpack them.

Robert Johnson has a useful guide to unpacking your dreams, called 'Inner Work', in which he details methods and examples to help.

In summary his four-step process is to look at:

1 Associations – associate your dreams to archetypes such as myths, fairy tales and ancient religious traditions, and be aware when an association 'clicks'.
2 Dynamics – Connect dreams inwardly to locate inner beliefs, attitudes and values, and subconscious personalities that define.
3 Interpretations – Choose alternatives that sit well with you, from which you can be closer to your subconscious reality.
4 Rituals – Do something to honor and incorporate the learnings from the dream. Light a candle, do *something*.

Johnson went on to say that the inner parts of our selves are clothed in images. These images Jung called 'archetypes' which are a way of identifying with an energy system or personality attribute that helps us to understand or create wisdom about our inner self.

In our unconscious we find our individual conception of God, and experience imaginings that act as a membrane between our conscious and unconscious. Here is a well-used example in the Nicene Creed, where it says, "I believe in One God". Johnson says that "*what this means psychologically is 'There is only one subject; there is only one source; one beginning; one unity out of which all the multiplicity of this life flows, and to which it returns*". The simple statement about One God thus carries an archetype of oneness which shows that though we seem to be individuals we are actually "plural beings' that share the collective psyche of the human race. Part of the evidence we have for the existence of the collective unconscious is that we find unconscious energies connect us to other people and to our entire environment; therefore, when we focus a great deal of energy within the inner world, a parallel energy often arises within the people or situations around us.

Because any dream is composed of energy systems, a good test for an interpretation is whether it connects to an energy behind it, in other words if UILE is part of it. If the interpretation arouses energy and strong feelings within you, if it suddenly gives you insights into your life, if it offers insights and liberates you from patterns you've been stuck in, all of these are signs that there is tremendous energy behind this interpretation.

Your dream's archetypes or symbols may be internationally understood, but unless the dream interpreter knows how you see them, and the dream interpretation sits well with you, then don't accept it.

Dreams are about your inner life. They are typically representing you in kaleidoscopic ways, with the intention of having you live a more abundant life. That is what dreams are about. The true message that will come out from interpretation will lead you towards a better, more authentic self. That may be a harsh message, requiring change, but listen for that message only.

Nebuchadnezzar was wrong in calling for his wise men to be killed because they could not interpret his dream. However, in many senses it is not a bad thing to expect the 'wise men' to be held accountable for their interpretations. Dream interpretation will depend on the base belief of the wise man. If a wise man believes that everyone is bad, then he will be looking for bad. If a truly wise man can see the treasure within, he will be looking to encourage you to dig within.

Summary

- Dreams are messages from your inner self.
- Dream messages are a treasure to be sought personally.
- The intention of dreams is to have you live a more abundant life.

Section Five – We Are All One UILE

> *Our country is the world, our countrymen are all mankind. We love the land of our nativity only as we love all other lands*
> From the 1838 Quaker declaration adopted by the Peace Convention

As I read the above quote I thought, "Wow! I am not alone in going past the artificial boundaries of lines drawn on a map, of distrust based on history of fear and revenge." We are all one. All humans are one species, one whole. Then I had to revise my thinking on why I divided or excluded anything. All life? All existence? Now it is time to consider how the Celtic concept of 'UILE' meaning all, everything, applies in how we approach the world, religion, art, community, science and ethics.

Chapter 19

Camel Drivers, Carpenters and Fisher folk

How did those priests ever get so serious and preach all that gloom?
I don't think God tickled them yet.
Beloved – hurry.
St. Teresa of Avila[82]

Sitting in a diverse group of people while discussing a topic of the heart, I am always blown away with the wisdom that is available. From the most educated to the most unlikely, the relevance and encouragement available is a source of great energy. It is the energy of wisdom, not science. Science informs us about knowledge of the material world, but wisdom and belief informs us of connection with the UILE that we truly are. Wisdom and knowledge are not in opposition, but wisdom has the wider scope to include that which we cannot explain, it includes that which is outside time, and that which provides meaning to how we live.

Wisdom has a deep sense of truth in it, which includes mystery. You see it is ridiculous for any one of us humans to believe we have all knowledge, though many may think they have inherited such all-knowing (omniscience) because of modern information banks. There is a big gap between knowing that information is recorded, and understanding it, absorbing it, and being able to investigate and touch a subject's perimeters. The older I get, the less I know, or the more I know that I don't know! Accepting our limited minds is the inverse function of understanding our unlimited connection through UILE. The concept of mystery starts with accepting our limited individual intelligence and our connectedness to infinite intelligence within the universe. It is relaxing into the whole, the holy.

Your true UILE self is not in opposition to science, quite the contrary, science is a subset of the whole mystery of life, namely that subset which explains what little we humans know about UILE's manifestation in the context of time. Science is awesome and expanding its reach daily into specializations of all kinds of wonderful knowledge. Don't kid yourself, though, science, though wonderful and huge, is just a fragment of the whole of wisdom. Einstein would agree. Here are three of his sayings: *"I want to know God's thoughts; the rest are details." "Science without religion is lame. Religion without science is blind." "Gravitation is not responsible for people falling in love."* True.

One of my favorite authors, Dr Rachel Remen, told the story of an experience with a case of terminal cancer which happened in a major teaching hospital where she was working. When the massive malignant cancer disappeared overnight a Grand Round was called and the case discussed. The doctors concluded it was a remission caused by chemotherapy which had been withdrawn a year prior. They concluded that this old therapy had suddenly taken effect, despite the fact the cancer had doubled during that same year! They did not want to admit to the mystery of what had happened.

Rachel herself took 15 years to appreciate that there was something outside knowledge that had occurred. She said, *"Mystery is a way of seeing. A moment where the mask of habit that makes things familiar, falls away. Mystery does not require us to do anything. Mystery may simply require us to see things in new ways, and remember to wonder. Maybe we all need to know a little less."*[83]

I would rephrase that last sentence of Rachel's to be, "Maybe we all need to understand how little we know, and despite our conscious ignorance we can more adequately live in wonder and abundance." You will never know everything, even of the fragment called science, but my wish for you is that you will increasingly understand wholeness, joy and your place within the mystery of UILE.

In her second marvelous book, *My Grandfather's Blessings,* Rachel wrote:

> *We do not serve the weak or the broken. What we serve is the wholeness in each other and the wholeness in life... Remembering this may require us to confront the core values of our culture.*
>
> *We are a culture that values mastery and control, that cultivates self-sufficiency, competence, independence. But in the shadow of these values lies a profound sense of isolation from our human wholeness. As individuals and as a culture we have developed a sort of contempt for anything in ourselves and in others that has needs, and is capable of suffering. In a highly technological world we may forget our own goodness and place value instead on our skills and our expertise. But it is not our expertise that will repair the world. Perhaps the future may depend less on our expertise than on our connection to one another and to life.*

Information grows exponentially, knowledge of what it means becomes more compartmentalized, and wisdom remains the stable domain of UILE.

It is in this light that we should have a look at the people who have most influenced the world for good. Think of the ones you respect and admire in history. Who were they? Jesus, Gandhi, Mother Theresa, Mohammed, Tolstoy, Buddha, Nelson Mandela and Martin Luther King are some of mine. What about yours? Are they respected for their knowledge or admired for the way they lived their life?

Consider the ones from whom the major religions were sourced. Did it matter what their expertise was, or was it their compassion and connection, their acceptance and love?

Jesus was a carpenter's son. He never had a book published; in fact there is no record of him even writing one. Mohammad, the prophet who founded Islam was a camel driver who found his message in a cave in silence. Buddha was a prince who renounced his worldly possessions once he discovered compassion for suffering. The Christian disciples were fishermen, probably never had any schooling, and yet like Mother Theresa they learned connection and became significant models for others.

What did Jesus say about those who had the equivalent of letters after their name? He said they needed to learn about caring for the poor and the widows, he taught them the importance of sitting with those they looked down on, and he preached love for enemies. These were significant messages that were sourced from an inner light, and then shone outward to others.

Of course we should learn and acquire knowledge in whatever way works for each individual. Personally I studied formally for over 25 years, but that was just a start because when learning stops, so does life. But how does learning help us to value our own being? Let me repeat what Rachel Remen said; *"In a highly technological world we may forget our own goodness and place value instead on our skills and our expertise."* Oprah Winfrey discussed a great example in her talk with Rob Bell in 2013, where a man who cleaned houses for a living understood the importance of his own self in the work he did, and in doing that inspired both of them. Simple authenticity often contains more energy than a lifetime of rushed, anxious and stressed days learning and doing.

However, is there a remnant of judgment within yourself when you look at people from different 'classes'? (Upper or Lower.) The judgment may come in the form of not wanting to listen to what they bring to the table. Sitting together and discussing important things, listening to alternative points of view, and spending time together provides a huge source of energy and understanding.

Community

Friends of mine work within the Initiatives of Change organization based in Caux, Switzerland. This organization structures meetings between Palestinians and Israelis, warring factions in the Great Lakes region of Africa, etc. In getting enemies together for week-long sessions sharing their stories, Initiatives of Change are helping to build trust and reconciliation. The stories are moving and inspirational, as people of different walks of life hear the other side of suffering, and change their point of view from anger to compassion.

So, where do people get the authority to lead in the field of compassion? Do they get a postgraduate degree in the subject? Is there training in a Seminary? Or do people look within and find it in silence? I think that the groups of people from all walks of life who support Initiatives of Change, and all outreach programs, find the energy within from a universal source of love.

Actually authority is not the issue with compassion anyway. Sharing brokenness is the source of true bonding. So it is with the priesthood of all believers, which is a Christian concept that no single role or person is the leader of the church, where the individual connection with love and the outflow of that love through compassion is the determinant of leadership.

Despite this, many religious leaders continue to harangue the general population with the intent of convincing that their theological way is correct, and should be followed. For a time I also was that way. How sad. The Negative-Ego has definitely got control of any person who believes they can speak on behalf of God, and you need to look at the consistency of message for those who attempt to give a helicopter view of what the universe is about. That is true for all sources of wisdom, including this book. Wisdom has always existed, so it makes sense that it would cross-reference between sources. Only take to heart those messages that sit comfortably with your soul.

It is our human nature and responsibility to share what we believe is good. It is our Negative-Ego nature to tell others what they should believe, in the process showing off our own internal need for some form of structure or control. It is better to look at why there is a dangerous inner desire to seek control, than to use our energies in promulgating some law or theology.

Letting go of the desire to control anything *other than your own being* is a good inner practice. All you need is love.

Summary

- It is not knowledge, but compassion in action, that your true soul aspires to.
- The energy of Love is available through everyone, camel drivers to carpenters and including you.
- Authenticity and a desire to hear the stories of others is a good place to start.
- Community is the training ground for the soul, but it requires exercising love!

Chapter 20

The Good Judge Meant

Judge not and you will not be judged
Luke 6:37

Condemnation and judgment are always a roadblock to self-growth.

Because UILE, the Supreme Spirit, is the instantiation of love, then love doesn't die, and it doesn't lie. Also what applies to one, applies to all.

So if the "no judgment" rule applies to the universe, then to make personal judgments is against ethical principle. You see, at the beginning, when we were created as spiritual beings, it was *with,* rather than *against* love. For heaven's sake, our creator was Love! If I hold the view that the universal creator is judging me for punishment, then modeling on that behavior I will judge myself too. However, as UILE is present within as part of my essential spirit, unconditionally accepting me, then if I don't love myself I will be rejecting all meaning. Can you see the difference?

There is no need for judgment which rejects each other or ourselves. Your intuition will show this is true. Deep inside you have a residual memory that informs you that you need to love yourself. Just be quiet and listen. It was the Negative-Ego that falsely led you to believe you were separate from other humans and UILE.

When we release ourselves from the tyranny of fear, and act in conscious care and compassion, we have no need to judge others. That is where God, as love, comes from. Yet our egos continue to judge, based on how we were taught, rather than on how we were born.

Let me give you an example. I made a mistake last year. I

trusted a guy in Ghana with a lot of my money to purchase land which appeared to be genuine, but was not. It is not an uncommon story throughout Africa I am told. However, the issue is that I judged myself and was down on myself for making that mistake, not having the wisdom to discern, and on not being able to put the money to better use.

As I whacked myself over the head, I was judging myself, and it took some serious quiet time to hear what the spirit was of this judgment. It was diminishing me.

Yet how do we learn other than by making mistakes? Does love reject because of mistakes? Would you reject your child for making a genuine mistake? I hope not, because love doesn't judge, it observes the experience, and just settles into acceptance – right now I cannot undo that mistake.

Sure, I did report it to the police, and am following up with action to retrieve the money, and yes there is such a thing as justice and judgment, but only for redressing societal laws. Courts in my experience never address matters of the heart or soul. In fact they can make matters worse.

Getting justice from a court is not going to undo my mistake. What lifts value from the mistake is learning forgiveness. I needed to forgive myself for my humanity, accept the grace and love of the Holy Spirit within, and move on.

Wayne Dyer says in one of his books that we need to look at the worst case outcome, assume that is what will happen, then from that place move forward and release our self-indictment. I did, and since then, though it still irks me, and I still have the ongoing consequences of legal action affecting my life, basically taking the position that the money won't return, I have let it go. It is, after all, just money. I didn't lose my love or my faith. I don't want to add another mistake to the first one, by losing my emotional and spiritual health in concentrating my energies on the past mistake.

Instead I am looking at what I have learnt, believing in my

self-worth, my sense of belonging as I am, with my frailties and mistakes. This means I can be positive for today, which will lead to a positive tomorrow.

Now I am working on not judging the people who have defrauded me – sure I cannot trust them, but I am trying now NOT to judge them for punishment, just accepting that consequences are an immutable law that will happen, reflecting back into their own lives, but does not diminish the spirit of worth which they were born with.

The last judgment is the point where I can give up judgment as a way of life, and so release myself from self-judgment also. Let's celebrate that, a Last and Final Judgment that we can be proud of!

To avoid judgment requires constant re-assessment of what you say and do. It is insufficient to assess that you are not prejudiced against race, color or creed. Life has a way of bringing others into your daily path, and each instance, from brushing against someone in a grocery aisle to counseling a good friend, has inherent challenges.

I have discovered that only by constant awareness and mindfulness can I discover the many ways I daily judge. It may be self-judgment regarding missing the opportunity to be helpful, the intentional turning away from someone who I find draining, negative thoughts regarding failure to adhere to healthy commitments, or a superior air with a child or someone with a disability. Doing a check to determine what the motives are behind can be exhausting and hard work, and that is why we often fail to judge our judgments! Yet it can become a way of observing, like a heads-up display that shows the modern fighter pilot where the enemy is, if you are willing to work at it. After that, a quick glance will inform you if your Negative-Ego is getting in the way of your intent to care for others.

Forgiveness

Once we have given up judgment, we have no condemnation, and therefore there is no need to forgive.

This is the simple rule then, of forgiveness. Forgiveness is the recognition of judgment, of exclusion, of labeling 'otherness' onto the criminal, the defrauder, the lawbreaker, the misunderstood, marginalized or the villain. Our goal is to release our judgment of being of different worth. When we acknowledge that we are only observers and do not know the whole story, our ability to accept is raised. Only once we accept our own brokenness, and our own potential to be in their place, can we accept that the human being behind any act remains holy, part of humanity as a whole.

Summary

- When we judge or label anyone we diminish both them and ourselves.
- Forgiveness is about taking off labels and seeing ourselves more clearly.
- No human being's soul can be defined by their behavior.

Chapter 21

Community Dreaming

In the path of your happiness shall you find the learning for which you have chosen this lifetime.
Richard Bach

What calls to you? What is the inspiration that you always drew from, and longed to spend your life at? Or are you working enslaved to obligation, courtesy of your Negative-Ego?

A Sense of Friendship

All of us desire the peace, freedom and relaxation that come when we leave the cocktail chatter and can relax with our intimate friends. Social expectations that caged us up like tigers inside the zoo of ourselves can be broken open, and, as Katy Perry sings, *"You're gonna hear me roar!"*

We don't have to keep up appearances. Our authentic selves can flow out to friends freely, and it is in giving from ourselves that we can actually find ourselves.

What is a friend?

- Someone who has your best interests in mind, who encourages you to be fully yourself, and loves you despite it!
- Duty and obligation do not have a place in true friendship. You don't have to act a play, or provide a service or payment for a friend. They are just so pleased to see you. This is the basis for a great sexual relationship too, that you want the other person's presence, without any obligation.
- The hallmarks of friendship are laughter and fun, warmth and intimacy, freedom and spontaneity without any

sacrifice to your own authenticity.

Friendship may also be the best definition of Love in action, because it is the inclusive energy that encourages you to know Love outside yourself. There is no point in UILE creating this entire complex universe from energy if there is no expression of Love, of itself.

MacMurray said, *"Neither knowledge nor beauty nor goodness can save or satisfy a single soul. Only friendship can do it. Friendship is the supreme value in life and the source of all other values."* Jesus' challenge is to not only be friends with our own bodies, but our neighbors, and our enemies. That is because we all share the same Spirit of UILE. If we are one, how can we take any other view?

Our challenge is to see UILE/God/the Great Spirit as our friend.

In the Christian faith the role of Jesus is that of friend, and true Christ-like behavior is to mirror his friendship. He did not turn away anyone, though he was able to state boundaries between his friendship and those who rejected his offers of acceptance and care. (Typically in the established synagogues/churches he rejected disrespect and lack of compassion for the poor etc.) He is a model friend and the teacher of friendship without barriers… In his footsteps we have a model friend who has left time, but still stands behind in principle and spirit. In the same way we can accept any other human, past or present, and respect their being. It does not mean we accept their behavior, their control, or their inherited beliefs and responsibilities.

Consider this story. Some years ago I had a work colleague called Pichai who lives in Thailand, and he felt an obligation to sweep the gravel at a Buddhist temple till his hands bled, in order to meet the requirements of compassion to allow his parents to be at peace…

The responsibility he felt caused physical harm, and it was ingrained into who he saw himself as. But *was* he responsible for others' lives in this way? He is probably still sweeping...

What is the responsibility to society or our families?

> *"Love is our true destiny. We do not find the meaning of life by ourselves alone - we find it with another."*
>
> Thomas Merton, *Love and Living*

There is a social aspect of responsibility, what our community expectations are, and a personal aspect, what we believe we are personally responsible for. Both involve relating to other people.

We cannot change social expectations, but we can critically review them. For example, in the case of abuse, society may say, "you must stand behind your family or spouse, no matter how they treat you", but this is wrong. In the case of physical abuse, it is pretty clear that a husband beating a wife, for example, is totally wrong and unacceptable. But it is also no different if the family member (father, wife, child, cousin or whoever) is intimidating. One story I heard was a guy who threatened his wife with a shotgun, he would blow her head off unless she did what he wanted. When she took this example to a counselor, the husband said, "yeah, but it wasn't loaded".

In both law and common sense, clearly this is abuse and assault.

Now as we slide along the scale from life-diminishing to life-enhancing behavior, we come across lots of abuse that is less obvious, but may be equally damaging.

So when a family member screams in anger, or hits out in frustration, or strikes a child, this is sometimes treated as acceptable behavior. It is not, ever, acceptable. A single instance may not be the direct reason to leave the relationship, e.g. for a child to leave home, for a wife to leave a marriage, but over time if this behavior does not change, it will sap life from both the abuser and the abused.

Now, what about further along the scale, where the behavior is constant nagging, or calling to find out where your spouse is because of jealousy and mistrust, or just calling and texting so much that the recipient cannot even think clearly, yet feels obliged to listen and respond.

This is still diminishing of life, and over time will break the relationship, either directly, or indirectly.

I wrote this poem in 2005, also about sweeping – talking about the feelings of obligation and being swamped with social expectation.

Sweeping leaves

I dreamed of a verandah
Covered o'er with falling leaves
And so many sad-faced sweepers
Wielding brooms to keep it clean.
But the wind was blowing.
The wind was winning,
puffing back the leaves,
Blowing back the leaves.
Futile activity
Of futile activities.
Then
I dreamed of the same people
Sitting in the leaves
Released
Happy.
Enjoying the breeze.

Sit back, and enjoy the leaves being in your life without feeling a pressure to sweep them, and your own sense of being, into a pile to be burnt. Relax!

Sweep those life-sapping obligations away, instead find

where life glows with rainbows!

The Persian poet Rumi wrote, "*Let yourself be silently drawn by the strange pull of what you really love. It will not lead you astray.*"

So, how to move from obligation to the freedom to do what you really love?

Firstly, you have to allow yourself to consider that you have potential, and that your wings will be carried on the wind which is other.

Secondly, contemplate on what you really want for your inner delight. What contribution can you make to the world, to others, that you will always get satisfaction from, even if it is a hard, difficult, even painful path.

Finally, you have to act and stop that procrastinating Negative-Ego from influencing you to not act on your life dreams. Like Ben Franklin, have an attitude of gratitude each day:

> *Oh powerful goodness! Bountiful Lord! Merciful guide!*
> *Increase in me wisdom that reflects my true desire and being. Strengthen my resolve to do what that wisdom uncovered. Accept what I play forward as a result of the ongoing blessings I receive.*
> Benjamin Franklin's daily prayer

So what about the obligations? Who will pay the bills? There is still a mountain of responsibility to climb. That is what Andrew said before starting the process of tackling his Negative-Ego. Andrew wanted to change his career, and get out of the political ugliness that his current workplace represented. In his mid-thirties, he had a wife and little girl, a large mortgage, and an expensive car. He asked how he could get away from what he called his 'slavery' of work, worry and women!

Once he stopped to even consider why he had entered this pattern, there were lots of questions that arose. Could he consider a lower cost lifestyle, a smaller house, a cheap car, and could his family accept less expenditure in the day to day and for yearly holidays? What was the thing he most wanted to do, that would inspire him? He had to learn to sit with his frustration, consider his loaded schedule, and consult with his wife. Then he remembered a dream. Two dreams actually. The first was a career dream that he got back in touch with from his childhood. He had wanted to be an ambulance driver and help people to safety. The second dream was during the night, when he dreamt that he was lifting a male friend out of a crowd of grasping people, all of whom were demanding money.

After analyzing these dreams he realized that his sense of self was submerged in his responsibilities, and that he needed to get back to what inspired him. He started to meditate 20 minutes a day, and he got the support of his wife to pursue his dreams. Over the next years they sold their large house and rented an apartment, allowing Andrew the breathing space to study for health. While he is not yet in the career he wanted, Andrew knows where he is going, and has learnt to believe in the power of intention. It has transformed his life, and he now views his work as a temporary way to earn money while he moves towards his life goal.

Richard Rohr said during his visit to New Zealand, "If you are not happy and joyful within yourself, you cannot claim transformation has happened to you."

Transformation is change in action, and it is transformation which is at the core of our journey home to ourselves. Being stuck or afraid is never part of our calling. We are asked to jump headlong into change, life, joy, abundance and the whole messy business of mystery. Yes, it will include pain, confusion, emotion and faith, these are as essential as the need to make decisions is. Decisions are not logical, they are us twisting and bucking in our attempts to unseat the ego riding us, and be free to run wildly with the wind in our manes.

Do you ever feel guilty for just sitting, or having fun? Try to buck that rider off, and experience true happiness.

Do you feel like work is slavery, that you are not doing what you feel you were called to be? Buck that rider off too.

Work can be part of the bliss of your calling, your contribution to love. Imagine waking up and being as excited to work as you were as a child waiting for Santa. Don't confuse the law and obligation of set work times with your calling. 9-5 work is not essential, spending time using your talents in a way that inspires you and others ***is***! Be open to change. But don't be surprised if your calling is what some may call boring or too hard. You can be inspired by so many alternatives, and you may mix a range of work options.

I love to do building construction work as well as write. One is very practical and I can see the outcome, and get fit at the same time while assisting others. The adventure of writing is based with paper or computer and doesn't provide physical exercise, but allows my imagination to soar. Both are wonderful, and of course I have many non-income hobbies and loves like music, philosophy and dance as well. These also are part of the package of what I see as heaven, abundant life here now.

Don't be narrow or constrained to a single task; look at the variety in the universe from which you were spawned. It is majestic in its complexity and awesome in its choices. Be part of it!

> *The same life-force that grows an oak from an acorn, a mountain from the earth's molten core, a stream from the spring thaw, a child from an egg and a sperm, an idea from the mind of a human being, is present in all things, all thoughts, and all experiences. There is no place where God is not.*
> Joan Borysenko

God is love. When we take up permanent residence in a life of love, we live in God and God lives in us. John 1 4:16

A Sense of Passion

Passion. It lies in all of us.
Sleeping... waiting... and though unwanted, unbidden, it will stir... open its jaws and howl.
It speaks to us... guides us. Passion rules us all. And we obey.
What other choice do we have? Passion is the source of our finest moments.
The joy of love... the clarity of hatred... the ecstasy of grief. It hurts sometimes more than we can bear.
If we could live without passion, maybe we'd know some kind of peace. But we would be hollow.
Empty rooms, shuttered and dank.
Without passion, we'd be truly dead.
Joss Whedon

Living life to the full definitely requires passionate involvement. It is a great word to describe oneness with what you are doing. But often it is used to refer to sexual passion. This is interesting, because the mechanistic approach would say we have intercourse in order to maintain the species, and that passion is just a side effect.

I believe the passion of sex is primarily relational – not procreational! It also has depth, and is mostly about connection and inner belief in your own lovability. As Gabriel García Márquez states, *"sex is the consolation you have when you can't have love."*

I think this is why sex is sold short, and making love is often missing. To me, sex is the expression of intimacy, touching and personalized care that takes friendship another step further. There is a trinity of sex, spirituality and friendship which all need to be present.

Without friendship, you have just a hormonal driven event, and it will never satisfy. There is a great chapter in Steve Biddulph's wonderful book *Manhood*[84] which describes sexual intimacy in a way that men particularly need to hear.

Without spirituality, there is no searching for the deeper person within, the one that is equally part of UILE, and without that connection, the connection is never as deep.

I believe the next stage of evolution requires free will in sexual objectives and friendship, reflected in the sense of family that bonds without obligation, based on the driving passionate motivation of love, in UILE.

Sometimes what is sweetest
can be right under your nose
But you still have to inhale
the fragrance.

Sometimes passion can be
bottled unnecessarily
in anticipation of a
good corkage in the future.

Our bottles were broken
last night.
Glass boundaries removed.
The two wines mixed in
intoxication.

Good signs for the new
vintage.

What about other passions, such as to thrill in the exhilaration of a rollercoaster, to eat a sublime meal, to create a work of art that seems to absorb every element of your being? All passions are about experiencing *intense*, even *overpowering* emotions.

Fascinating.

Life in all its fullness, abundance, and bliss, is life on the edge where you feel your being will actually flood out it is so strong. Anger, joy, excitement, it doesn't matter the type of emotion, this is deep penetrating involvement in life. Soldiers sometimes talk about being in battle and the emotional intensity being so strong that they feel 'alive' in a way they had never experienced before.

Fascinating, because that energy, that intensity, is like a hug or an embrace from UILE. In the experience of passion there is connection to a deep awareness of UILE, and because the connection is so strong, you become aware of your divine nature. Focus on a time when you felt like this. Did you feel like you could do anything at that point?

Next time you soak in the pool of passion, pay attention! You are the iceberg in the sea of UILE, remember!

A Sense of Humor

When you come to a fork in the road; take it
Yogi Berra

Humor is extreme creativity producing an unexpected outcome.

"There was a man talking to God, trying to get God's perspective on things.

The man says to God, "What is a billion years like to you?"

God says, "A second."

The man says, "Oh that's interesting. Well then, what is a billion dollars like to you?"

God replies, "A penny."

The man, with his materialist Negative-Ego cutting in, thinks to himself "Hey, if a billion dollars is like a penny to God then a million must really be trivial!"

So the man asks God, "Can I have a million dollars, then?"

God's response is fast, "Sure… Just wait a second!"[85]

Humor categorized:

- A funny situation, such as when you observe something which is wildly incongruous like a sheep riding a bicycle, juggling a "Wear more wool" sign! When the Dalai Lama met Bishop Tutu at a Peace Conference, they hugged, and then proceeded to tickle each other till they were both laughing. That is true humor, it has unexpected life within it.
- Funny jokes always have a dual or unusual ending – the punch line. What did the mystic say to the hot dog vendor? Make me one with everything.
- Humorous conversation is when the topic, noises and environment are different to the participant's sense of being inappropriate, fun, irrelevance and at play. E.g. making fun of Shakespeare: *"What's in a name, anyway? That which we call a nose by any other name would still smell."*

Art can hold whimsical humor as well – consider this from Hafez; "First the fish needs to say: Somethin' ain't right about this CAMEL ride... and I'm feeling so damned thirsty."

I am bringing humor and laughter to your attention because all life is unpredictable, and humor is one way to bring attention to everyone's basic need to play. When we laugh we are always getting in touch with our inner child in a fun way. Elvis Presley once said about laughter, *"It's pure freedom. It's like being a kid again."* True, and I will always be a kid at heart.

UILE is the creator of all diversity, and nature abounds in humor. Play is a key way to regain some of the wild joy inherent in your UILE nature.

This is a poem about that natural humor.

The scope

The scope is huge –
Too huge for a specialist to know
even a fragment.

The best human minds fight over understanding
one genome, in one cell,
while generations of viruses run uncheck'd.

UILE is behind it all, in it all, beyond the bickering.

With each discovery the scope expands,
making previous wisdom seem child-like,
though finding eternal truths were known
more in the past, than in the arrogant present.

No lack of information now,
Information just fuels the scope, or perspectives of it.

and UILE smiles.

The laws of nature are boxed into book sets
and published in condensed form for all to understand.

and UILE sniggers.

The scope increases exponentially
as the limited grasp of individuals
in their ivory silos.

and UILE laughs,
and guffaws.

And one who sits and is open to the womb
of the scope,
has a revelation,
a dream.

And in the dream

UILE is laughing still.
And the universe
jiggles in her belly
from the laughter.

Ready to be borne.

Summary

- Life is for relationships of joy.
- Friendship is the best form of religion, love one another.
- Love with passion, true love is never about obligation.
- There are some things you cannot have too much of. [86]
- Love loves laughter.

Chapter 22

UILE in Science, Art and Spirituality

Science and religion are not concerned with two different worlds but with one and the same world – the only world there is.[87]
Prof John MacMurray

Creativity consists of allowing UILE to flow, because it is modeling the source of all creativity.

The energy of creativity, and joy, comes from the delight of loving what you are doing right now, and every moment that you encounter as you experience time. Your emotions reflect the messages from UILE, you choose to act from the clarity of peace and joy, and because Love's delight is in the action.

Let's consider work for example. When I was directing Unique Software, a company that built enterprise level solutions for the international market in the 1980s, I met with each of my staff on a monthly basis. Because we were a creative company, and small, I relied on the enthusiasm of the staff. Consequently, if they were not excited to come to work I encouraged them to take the day off and figure out what needed to happen in order to regain the enthusiasm to contribute eagerly to our objectives. In other words I assumed that they had the same level of personal identification with their daily work as I did! (They may not have, but the principle is that creativity is best achieved when you love what you are doing.)

The energy within UILE is wild and creative, but our societal systems attempt to constrain that by invoking the Negative. The next sub-sections give some insight into how Education, Art and Science are affected.

Art

True art awakens the
Extraordinary
Ovation
Hafez, *The Gift*

Art arrives as creativity in life, however science and art are fragmentary and, though both can be inspirational, they only deal with slices of reality, not the big picture of meaning.

To explain this further, you may hear a piece of music and be moved, but the music will resonate with some, not others. Holistic reality is applicable to everyone, everything. The intent of true art is to spark some emotional or imaginative chord and through that spiritual connection open the channel to wisdom or love. The spark is valuable, but it is not the flame. Indeed the spark may trigger Negative-Ego reaction. For example, a novelist's characters may be vicious or feeble, a painting may portray an act of violence, so art is not bound by morality; it may in fact shock the receiver into considering ugliness.

John MacMurray says that, "a living work of art strikes always at the roots of our complacency and its beauty is hidden by its attack upon our security and our traditions."[88]

Filling up with beauty
Like soothing water between the hard fact-rocks of life,
beauty infiltrates, if you let its
shimmering emerald diaphanous silk
polish your soul-space.

Along the exotic sand-dunes of today
tracking bitter thirst without meaning or place
and without open air, without sand in the teeth
a sense of reality in an LCD screen,

beauty is flowing in a rippling stream
when the moment is taken to lever
the eyes away from fish-bowl media.

But to reach this distant planet of truth
requires a journey of concentration
never experienced by primitive forebears
To tear the eyes away from the sexy packaging,
the instant revenge of frags in a first-person-shooter play,
the jangle of the coins running into the tray,
the more-more-more of the gigantic store,
the CGI graphics of fantasy in world always offering more,
the arm-pulling attention of the mobile phone,
or the clamor of the far-from-reality show,
is a quest that demands more
than ever before.

I am sure the Lawrence (of Arabia fame),
took time to experience the simple ripples of sand
worn by the serpent of wind.
And so I imagine young Tutankhamun
amazed by the tallest of pyramids and
even more by his mother's soft limbs.

And where are the heroes today?
who can say?
Could media stars pray
in obeisance to some other god
than themselves? No way.
And would they know beauty
if they sat in a vat of it?

The fact is that heroes are those
I suppose ,

are right under our nose:
who can find golden beauty in a pond or a smile,
who can fill up with rose-views,
or miles and miles of forests or beach.
True heroes of beauty reflect on the simple,
the everyday fur of a pet, a gold beetle.
They have the knack
to appreciate wrinkles on forehead,
a laugh-line,
a skin-curve,
a soft lip,
a promise."
Philosofree

MacMurray goes on to state that *"art is the spontaneity of the personal, the expression of self, the creation of the vision of what might be real, and therefore the architect of the future."* I agree, and it is for this reason that we should use art to trigger our connectedness with UILE, via the spontaneity of play, the self-expression of imagination, the dreaming of what may be possible, and hence the participation in architecting a future that is beyond time.

As explained in Chapter 8 above, creativity is a messenger for UILE, and I believe that all creativity relies on UILE as its source.

Science

There is a demand for a religion that modern science need not be ashamed to serve[89]

Science grows out of our understanding of material things. Like the story of the three blind men describing an elephant, each person has a different view of science. The elephant is indeed a marvel and worth the investigation, however, our understanding is constrained by our Negative-Ego, and limited by our intellect and the inability to focus on any more than one part of the whole at a time. For that reason, history has shown that no scientific statement can ever be final. Science forms the illusion that we know more than we do.

Thomas Kuhn in his 1960's book *The Structure of Scientific Revolutions* explained why science is not simply devoted to the rational pursuit of truth, but is and will continue to be subject to human foibles, ambitions, emotions, and peer-group pressures. It is a form of belief which is just as full of Negative-Ego as right-wing religious fundamentalism.

An example of the danger to free thought is the recent (2011) creation of a 'Guerrilla Skepticism on Wikipedia' team who modify the contents of Wikipedia with the aim to discredit those who place views which show how science is full of anomalies, such as the claims of Robert Sheldrake, a prominent biologist. Sheldrake argues in his work that the basic premises of science are beliefs that are no more supportable by evidence than the paranormal. Those like the Guerrilla Skeptics are so defensive of their position that they try to ban thought, much like during the Spanish Inquisition. In fact during an episode of Heretics of Science, a documentary broadcast in the UK in 1994 repeatedly displayed footage of book burning, sometimes accompanied by audio of a crowd chanting "heretic". It is the same control behavior that has repeated during history whenever a line of belief is questioned, and it shows how the materialist fringe is just as afraid of variant thinking as the religious fringe. Consider the withdrawal from the TED website of the video of Sheldrake's challenge to scientific assumption. If science is always factual, just truth, and not belief, what is there to fear by having people question it?

Because science cannot show us values, ideals, or morality, a scientific age is always a materialistic age. For that reason Immanuel Kant concluded: "*my great work is destroying reason to make room for faith*".

I would like to point out that I truly believe in science as the empirical method for best practice in collecting and categorizing knowledge. However, the empirical method for best practice in collecting and categorizing wisdom is the observation of personal relationships. My observation of wisdom over history is that those who are wise draw people to them through love and compassion, and tend to have an inspiring acceptance of science and life in general. The opposite is not true. I know scientists who are experts in their field but are unsuccessful in relationships. Knowledge may open minds, but it does not open hearts.

The conclusion for me is that wisdom is living love, and that this practice provides the abundance that cannot be found in science. Equally though, science is a contributor to the abundance, and should be considered an ally of wisdom. I think this age is bringing humanity to an awareness of how wisdom and knowledge can be equally respected. My belief is that UILE wisdom informs a spirituality that modern science need not be ashamed to serve.

Education

Paul Simon expressed a frustration that many can relate to; *"When I think back on all the crap I learned in high school, it's a wonder I can think at all."*[90] It would be illogical to not recognize the problems in our education system. As Jordan and Raymond P. Shepard explained:

> *Because it has not defined the nature of man, education is in the untenable position of having to devote its energies to the development of curricula without any coherent ideas about the nature of the creature for whom they are intended.*

I agree. We are spiritual beings in a temporal body, yet our education systems are all based around materialistic views of the world, at the same time that science is saying that mystery is an integral part of the equation.

Einstein wrote, "*The only thing that interferes with my learning is my education*." If that educated man could say that a hundred years ago, would it not apply even more today?

The structure of modern society is often reliant on education being provided by non-family during each child's formative years. This means that individualistic opinion is reduced. The kind of 'we have the truth' thinking that comes from radical science and religious proponents is subject to the Educational hierarchy's dogma at the time. Science is essential, so is spirituality, and neither should be denied in the upbringing of balanced individuals. We have leant too far away from honesty. It is our duty to educate with the premise that despite our vast increases of knowledge, we still can only define a small part of what is important in life.

Most of the critical stuff is still mystery, and that includes science. Telling our children that we *know* that memories are stored in our brains[91], or that we *know* that the universe was formed in an instant from *nothing* during the Big Bang (and yet we are sure that energy can never be created), is much the same thing. Science has some religious beliefs that are no more substantial than spiritual beliefs. Ignorance and boundaries should be admitted.

It is the role of wisdom thinkers to question, and to teach how to question, which is an important role.

I lament for the loss of direct one-on-one tutoring which offers relationship, connection and true joy in learning from inspiration and work together. Teachers do a sterling job, but those with a class of 25-30 children are not in a position to optimize learning by one-on-one joint tasking. Would this make a difference? Consider the case of Helen Keller, born blind and deaf in 1880. With the commitment of 20-year-old Anne Sullivan, herself visually impaired, to become Keller's instructor, Helen was the first deaf-blind person to achieve an arts degree.

Working together, (Anne was also visually impaired) Helen was able to transcend all known concepts of learning to become a loved author, political activist, and lecturer.

Helen tellingly wrote: *"Alone we can do so little; together we can do so much."*

Education is so necessary, but we cannot be complacent about the way it affects our children's lives. In the Lakota Way[92], "elders were the first to tell children and remind everyone that the pursuit of knowledge must be a lifelong endeavor. Interestingly enough, an elder would be the first to tell you that he or she really did not know much." Our Education system could do with such humility. Knowing a lot in a specific silo or specialist field doesn't improve your life, it is the connection to meaning, to who you truly are and want to give that is the key. "I think, increasingly, anything you learn is going to become obsolete within a decade," said Lawrence Summers, a former president of Harvard University, "and so the most important kind of learning is about how to learn." It is such openness that also allows you to follow your true life 'bliss' occupation. You are always open to your dreams if you 'learn how to learn'.

In Robert T. Kiyosaki's book, *If You Want to Be Rich and Happy, Don't Go to School: Ensuring Lifetime Security for Yourself,* he argues that the western education system is damaging because it misses or even teaches against the following essential knowledge:

- Generalized principles: Students should acquire a set of generalized principles that will allow them to apply them to diverse situations.
- Principles of money, business and finance: Students should learn about these principles so that they can be prepared for the practical realities of adult life.
- Freedom of choice: Students should be allowed to pursue their interests in their work. The freedom of choice taps into the intrinsic passion of learning within students.

- Life-long learning: Learning is a perpetual process that does not end when people leave school. Instead of focusing on getting increased pay, people should be concentrating on acquiring knowledge.

However, I think mass education system is lacking a lot more than these points, as:

- it does not typically teach about how to learn by watching and copying a respected individual.
- It implies that knowledge is what is necessary to succeed, further encouraging the totally false myth that supports stinking thinking, that what you are told defines who you are. What is necessary for a rounded education is that mystery, not Harry Potter, but true mystery and the boundaries of science are introduced. Can this be done in traditional schools? I doubt it.
- It does not know how to teach virtues, spirit and friendship, and ways to interpret what is ethical life instead of pushing the materialism barrow.

Einstein again: *"Education is what remains after one has forgotten everything he learned in school."*

Consider teaching your children outside the school system, if possible. Explain to them that school is just a start. I am suggesting teaching more than the essential curricula of *readin', writin' and arithmetic*. I do believe that secondary school subjects have value in them, but the value is mined mainly when the student becomes aware in themselves of their desire and passion to learn. This is the primary reason why individual training inspires. It allows for the injection of care and inspiration into the student.

Finding wisdom, on the other hand, is a process of attending to the present, in other words spiritual awareness, and I think it is the family responsibility, not the teacher, to do this job. Each parent can demonstrate by their own daily practice how:

- to sit quietly and respect silence, darkness and mystery,
- to focus on their own body and keep it fit and healthy,
- to listen with awe to a song, to read a book with passion to their child,
- to listen with empathy to the emotional turmoil that the child brings home from their school day,
- to recognize UILE in their pet dog/cat, and
- to encourage the imagination to run wild.

Spirituality is the living of abundance in your life as part of UILE. You are not alone. You have meaning. Your hope is a bud from the plant of faith in your spirituality, and the flower from this plant is joy, peace and abundance.

Health Systems

I worked in a western public hospital for 14 years, and during that time there were constant calls to move from repair to prevention. Rather than the majority of health effort going towards pumping pills, or cutting up bodies, all major health strategists agree that prevention is a more effective use of money. It is just that health systems don't do it, because they are not set up that way. Imagine if health providers were allocated clients and paid based on their health indicators.

There are also eastern approaches to health. The Japanese Reiki healing method balances and focuses energy. Reiki translates as Universal Life-Force Energy, Rei meaning Universal energy, Ki meaning life-force energy.

The earliest record of Indian Ayurvedic medicine dates from around 2500 BCE. The word Ayurvedic comes from two Indian words, Ayur meaning life and Veda meaning knowledge. Ayurvedic or life knowledge medicine is based on how to lead a healthy, balanced life. Balanced life is interpreted as balance between spiritual and physical, and this medical approach names the non-physical body as the 'subtle body'. Ayurvedic medicine observes illness as unevenness in the body, which may be treated with a mixture of meditation, physical exercise and herbal treatments. This approach appears more balanced than the western emphasis on drugs and pathology.

Chakra means vortex, spinning wheel or Mandala. Chakras are considered the major centers of spiritual power in the human body, as locations or energy portals through which the energies of our subtle body life flow into our physical body to give balance.

You may have wondered if instead of going to a hospital or clinic, you could affect your own health, and start a revolution as an individual. I did too, and these are a couple of simple, but effective, recommendations. Move and Focus.

Move

Western society in general is moving less, both in quantity and quality. Let me tell my story. Many years ago I commonly had severe back pain, not surprisingly since I was at a desk for eight plus hours a day. I went to remediation, and sometimes it relieved the pain, usually for a short time. Long ago I decided to follow the principles of "Touch for Health" which advise that regular yoga-like stretching will ensure that the tightened muscles were released.

To cut a long story short, I did the exercises regularly and found that after a few months of regular work the back pain went away indeed! Being a little slow to learn, I stopped doing the exercises, the pain returned, and I resumed, etc. In short, by moving every muscle in your body on a regular basis (and there were a lot I discovered that I hadn't even known existed) they become stretched and pliable. That means that tension pressures on the skeletal system were removed, and the body returned to its planned balance. I now do yoga every few days and am fitter, more flexible and healthier.

I won't discuss the concepts of chi (Qi) and energy here, but as mentioned in chapter 1, Qi is a Chinese term for "natural energy", "life force", or energy flow". Qi is also the central underlying principle in traditional Chinese medicine and martial arts. I wonder if those who wrote about Qi recognized its intention and its pervasiveness across the universe, its implicit love of life. I suspect so.

Focus

The next example is about my knee. I played Australian Rules Football when I was young, and because it is a rough sport, I broke my ankle and caused significant damage to my left knee. My ankle healed well, but as the decades rolled by my knee became painful, and indeed at times crippling.

Some time ago I did remedial work on the knee, to build up the muscle around it. That helped. However, at times I would still have pain, and so I decided to put my belief in energy to the test. After experiencing crippling pain, I chose to focus the energy which is within my body, my UILE source, to the location of my knee. I did this regularly, just concentrating my body onto the left knee. To my surprise, it worked! OK, I should have had more faith, I understand that, but I learnt from the experience. Energy can be focused.

Soon after, I spoke with a friend in the UK who pointed out that a whole lot of study is now going into focusing energy as a means of healing. Not just the chi I mentioned above, but of mental direction of the energy within. Contemplating the various chakras is useful and a good practice to focus on the aspects of the subtle body.

The chakras are aligned along the spine and can be defined as:

1 Root Chakra - body survival, strength of character,

patience, endurance and safety.

2 Sacral Plexus – sexuality and sensuality, physical force, open-mindedness, our ability to yield and cooperate.
3 Solar Plexus – energy and self-control, emotional issues and issues of self-acceptance.
4 Heart – forgiveness, compassion, empathy, trust, equilibrium and ease with our life.
5 Throat – communication, dreaming, artistic expression, good judgment, self-belief, wisdom, truthfulness.
6 Brow – intuition, imagination, visualization, concentration, insight, enlightenment; it also defines fantasy and reality.
7 Crown – spiritual will, inspiration, idealism and connection with the universe.

There are many resources that describe the chakras and the subtle body. For example, I refer you to Caroline Myss' book *Anatomy of the Spirit* which allocates a chapter for each of the 7 chakras. It is good practice to contemplate ways of understanding your being. Other good toolsets are the Enneagram which is described on http://www.enneagraminstitute.com, Myers-Briggs Personality Test (http://www.myersbriggs.org/my-mbti-personality-type/mbti-basics/) and several other psychological and management based on the 'Big 5' personality traits. There is understandable similarity in the tests and outcomes, no matter what the background.

I agree with what Richard Rohr says, "For many of us, the body is more *repressed and denied* than even the mind or the heart. It makes both presence and healing quite difficult, because the body, not just our mind, holds our memories."[93] We all need to remember to honor our physical needs, while we experience life in time.

Focusing is spending time with what is directly here, but not clear. Let go of your need for perfection, assurance and control.

Let the power of UILE be the mystery it will always be, connect to Love in the way you fall in love.

> *Authenticity is a collection of choices that we have to make every day. It's about the choice to show up and be real. The choice to be honest. The choice to let our true selves be seen.*
> Brené Brown, *The Gifts of Imperfection: Let Go of Who You Think You're Supposed to Be and Embrace Who You Are*

Don't be afraid of mystery, if an experience is not clear but makes life more abundant, why would we not do it?

Summary

- Knowledge is based on beliefs that change.
- Art is the flowering of UILE's creativity within you.
- Scientific thought is no more valid than philosophical thought, question everything, trust people, not theories.
- Think about new models for educating yourself and your children.
- Move and Focus for good health.

Chapter 23

Returning Home Free

When we focus on others, our world expands. Our own problems drift to the periphery of the mind and so seem smaller, and we increase our capacity for connection – or compassionate action.
Daniel Goleman, *Social Intelligence: The New Science of Human Relationships*

The energy of love can be aligned for good just like meridians of the body, like Feng Shui or the placement of a rock in a Buddhist temple. That is the purpose of religion – a society that is aligned to love each other. That was the message of Jesus, Mohammed, Buddha and of the Tao.

Maybe the trillions of stars and planets in the universe are just a mirror of the cells in your body, and we can join the creator in laughing at our smallness.

Maybe space is a place that exists everywhere love is, and we look at a sky filled with the wind of love, shining with the pink glow of dawn for those who are awake.

Maybe we are all connected via a single collective unconscious intelligence, the universal mind of UILE, and our restlessness is UILE's inner messengers calling us to pay attention.

Maybe your life has a meaning – to be in harmony with love and joy. But you misplaced the key to set you free. Or it was hidden as a game to make life interesting.

Here are some attitudes that will help bring you home; free!

Embrace Yourself

Your task is not to seek for love, but merely to seek and find all the barriers within yourself that you have built against it.
Rumi

When we love something it has our concern, our attention, its welfare is in our heart. Yet Negative-Ego often creates a view of self that leads us to follow others' points of view, that we should be 'selfless' (i.e. be good slaves to another's wishes), that we should 'ignore our sinful needs, especially emotional or hormonal' (i.e. don't pay attention to what is going on inside, and that we should 'love others before ourselves' contrary to the rule which every flight promotes, namely "pull down the oxygen mask and place it on yourself first, before attending to those around you").

"Don't forget to love yourself."
Soren Kierkegaard

You cannot love someone else with abundance and freedom if you have not attended to your own inner needs. I am not saying this about material things, St. Francis gave away all his wealth and it was a blessing to him. This is about spending the time to embrace your own being, to recognize UILE within, to respect that, then to go on, and from that starting point to spend time regularly on your physical health, your spiritual journey, and your emotional and psychological needs. It seems so logical that it should be unnecessary to say it. But most of us battle with this issue of loving ourselves, because we were taught we were bad, unworthy, difficult etc. Burney says, "Learning to love ourselves, and remembering that the God-Force loves us, is what will bring peace within."

Everyone expects and wants love.

Do you accept that you have to give love in order to attract it into your life? However, you can't give what you don't have. The only way forward for this world is to discover that the love inside you is already there, and it provides a connection to the source of UILE. Once this truth is admitted you can relax and concentrate on being yourself, for in your joy and daily passion you will automatically draw from the deep well of Love inside.

As Lucille Ball from the Iconic *I Love Lucy* show said, *"Love yourself first and everything else falls into line."*

Embracing yourself involves accepting your value and worth, and following your own inner guidance system, which itself is part of UILE.

Embrace Change

Security is mostly a superstition. It does not exist in nature, nor do the children of men as a whole experience it. Avoiding danger is no safer in the long run than outright exposure. Life is either a daring adventure, or nothing.
Helen Keller

"Let your home be your mast and not your anchor."
Kahlil Gibran

The one constant is change. Yet we run from it, from its personification as fear, hiding in the vain hope that it will not catch us. But change is another word for energy. UILE is always changing, creating, moving and inspiring us towards the new. What if instead of running away, we hold our arms wide to change when it visits us? We will not fall, we will encounter the embedded humor, the embrace of the creator of all things new, and during change we will shrug off the suffocating chrysalis of Negative-Ego and emerge in flight and beauty into an abundant butterfly day.

Richard Rohr summarises the recurring themes in all of the world's religions and philosophies:

- There is a Divine Reality underneath and inherent in the world of things,
- There is in the human soul a natural capacity for, similarity to, and longing for this Divine Reality, and
- The final goal of existence is union with this Divine Reality.

This is the Divine Reality of UILE, of a bigger concept of an all-embracing, all-encompassing, all-energy yet personally intimate God that transcends life, death, joy and pain, time and eternity.

Rob Bell tells a story about seeing a vehicle accident where a woman was knocked from her bicycle and he ran to help, to discover that life is holy, precious.

He went on to say,

> The gift of life can be taken from you at any moment. When you talk about God it generally veers into you have to believe or do or say the right stuff. So God becomes, who is right, who is wrong, who is in, who is out, who is with us, who is not. This takes us down the road which does not help, does not bring life and actually has made the world a much worse place. It is one thing to have the furniture in your brain arranged correctly, but it is another thing to see. I guarantee that the people you most respect, who you most want to be like, are the people who see, and when you are with them, something about their presence, you slow down. Something about the way he or she cooks, it slows you down, and you are reminded of peaceful things.[94]

Life may appear small; it may seem mundane, with repetitive activity, sickness, constraint, staleness or lack of adventure. However, even in apparent banality, there can be the abundance of a magnificent life. A day spent baking, or cutting concrete, if done with love, with the enthusiasm that sparkles in wide eyes, is a magnificent day. A day as president of the world or the stage, pushing buttons of execution in a tower of control, or flashing smiles of anonymity, is far less impressive to me, because it is how our hearts operate that shows how magnificent our real being is. The next person you meet, who could be a broken shell in a wheel chair, or a depressed criminal, may be the one who can lift you to heights you never imagined.

It is one thing to be right, now, it is another thing entirely to be here right now, being present to the guest you have in front of you. In every moment, of abundance, of creativity, of joy, of laughter, there is change. Embrace it.

Embrace Solitary Contemplation

> *Our reality, our true self, is hidden in what appears to us to be nothingness... We can rise above this unreality and recover our hidden reality*
>
> Thomas Merton, *New Seeds of Contemplation*

In my experience just getting time alone to think about meaning, to listen to the messengers from within, and to process the messages from without, that is solitary contemplation. You don't have to become a hermit or a monk, you don't have to chant, you don't have to force yourself to sit for hours in a yoga position. You don't have to do anything that doesn't work for you. That is the voice of Negative-Ego resisting the inward pull of UILE.

Instead of ordering yourself to concentrate, to start or stop thinking in a certain way, which is a typical newbie approach to 'doing' contemplation, just relax, allow yourself to 'fall into yourself' and then just pay attention to your inner messengers, note your dreams (*it's ok to make notes*), attend to your emotions (*even if it means a rollercoaster ride for a while*) and don't be afraid to let your imagination take over. Daydreaming is not forbidden, there are no rules here. Whatever brings you closer to mining what is *below* your conscious 'doing', which is your true 'being', is where the richest mother lode is found.

We are so busy that we don't make time to focus on what is going on inside. We may be unaware that depression has seized us that something good is developing inside; a new strength emerging, a wound healing, or a chronic fear evaporating. This happens when we have not tackled honest assessment of our faith.

We all begin our lives with a set of attitudes that are dictated to us by the world outside us. If we are consciously aware of them as our beliefs, we assume that they are right, it rarely occurs to us to question them. But faith, personal faith, cannot be inherited or passed down, as Kierkegaard said. Each person must claim their authentic faith. This requires effort, because to behave ethically requires an honest assessment to determine consistency of your behavior to your values. Faith therefore requires questions which prod you back to who you really are, not ignorance and dumb acceptance of external points of view. Robert Johnson points out that, "*it is worth pure gold to know what you are really up to, underneath your professed ideals.*"

If you ethically want to know meaning, it requires action to dig deep inside, to spend time looking for your true self, to claim your own cloak of faith, not the inherited one you put on by default. The source is UILE, and faith is found by balancing between inner (contemplative) and outer (conscious thinking) awareness. These yin and yang aspects are not right and wrong, they are integral aspects of being. Johnson explains:

> *The unconscious attitude is always off-center exactly to the same extent that the conscious ego is (to the other side). As the ego attitude becomes more moderate, the unconscious attitude also relaxes toward the center. The attitude that is your true self, lies*

> *somewhere in between.*

Thomas Keating suggested that:

> contemplative practices make one vulnerable to the unconscious, so that the undigested emotional material of a lifetime, the trauma that we couldn't face as children, that we repressed into the subconscious that is stored in the nervous system and the body, are still lingering there with their energy and influencing our decisions and attitudes that can be processed. The ego is opposed to such contemplative practices.

I like the concept of embracing your soul, putting your arm around the eternal nature of who you truly are, and befriending it. You *are* at one with UILE, even if you may not feel like it just now. Befriend your inner baby that was you before you left your mother's womb, befriend your inner child that still had glimpses of the eternal joy in creative play, and forgive your past, it is no longer relevant for who you truly are.

Alfred North Whitehead once said that, "religion is what the individual does with his own solitariness... and if you are never solitary, you are never religious."

Holding nothing, being empty and quiet so that there is space to be filled, that is when we are also embraced by the Spirit of UILE.

> *Learn to get in touch with the silence within yourself, and know that everything in this life has a purpose. There are no mistakes. No coincidences. All events are blessings given to us to learn from.*
> Elizabeth Kubler-Ross

The opposite of solitary is of course the cult of 'being popular'. Did you know some people today evaluate their worth on the basis of the number of hits they get on social media?

It is so modern to impose a sense of self-blame regarding social responsibility for connecting with remote people via email, Facebook. Self-blame is never helpful, especially if it is for silly reasons. No wonder modern Westerners feel pressure and lack of time. The devil is in the detail; in this case in feeling obliged to send birthday messages to people we hardly know just because of an electronic reminder!

Think also about mobile phones! Their arrival has resulted in codependency and lack of confidence. Give me one reason why it is not a denial of trust to expect to know the location of a loved one every few hours. In the case of a child the message is that disconnection and independence is dangerous. In the case of a partner it is poisonous distrust or a form of stalking by media.

Worse still is that your negative-ego may be thinking it is a benefit. From five years old I walked or rode to school and no, it was not statistically safer then. These expectations are new and, like the thinking you can prevent harm by proximity, wrong. The biggest dangers to you and your children are in fact those you know, probably those who are in fact empowered by the same media you think will protect you.

I see kids shriveling in fear from walking down a normal road, parents trying to cover every possible moment of a child's life and causing overall more damage than the feared accident or rare acts of evil. Most people are like you, loving and kind. Don't warp your perspective to fit in with the news that shows one awful event and refuses to balance that with the hundreds of thousands of warm, kind and protective events that surround you each day.

One of the major advantages of solitary meditation is that it removes you from concentrating on the ego, and if it is open to an awareness of UILE, replaces the rush and bother of media with a deep sense of gratitude and connection.

Embrace Others

When you meet anyone, remember it is a holy encounter. As you see him, you will see yourself. As you treat him, you will treat yourself. As you think of him, you will think of yourself. Never forget this, for in him you will find yourself, or lose yourself.

Marianne Williamson, *Broken Open – A Return to Love*

I had an 'Aha' moment this week. It was about who our neighbor is. You may recall that Jesus once said, "Love your neighbor as yourself." The question his disciples wanted answering was "who is our neighbor?" Of course it is more than just the person in the house next door. I discovered it is primarily the person who is physically near at this present moment. "Aha" I thought. It is the stranger at the bus stop who drops their shopping bag, your son or daughter calling for assistance with homework, a workmate who is angry with you for some reason, anyone you bump into. These are the embraces of the daily life, the 'holy encounters' that Marianne Williamson is referring to above.

In those cases where you do know the person on your path, if it is possible and socially appropriate, touch them. Shake their hand. Hug your relatives. On YouTube there are many great videos of people giving out 'FREE HUGS' in a public square. Look at the smiles on the recipient's faces! There are few things so healing as a giving hug. Touch is so important. Your skin is a membrane to life, and life energy transfers in and out through that membrane. When you give out, you get back. Hugs, like compliments, actually activate dopamine hormone release that creates a sense of well-being. Not only do the recipients get a gift of dopamine, but recent studies have shown that observers of such a loving act also get a similar dopamine rush. That includes the giver. So trade a hug for some dopamine today!

Seriously, though, relationship is not an optional part of life. We are all one, all UILE. Collective unconscious, the mind of

UILE, is dependent on the individuation of each one of us. If we want to participate in this process it is not by changing others, it is by looking inside to find the relationship with UILE, with 'All', with wholeness. This in turn results in finding a source of energy inside which encourages and empowers us to embrace each other. Embracing each other helps conquer the Negative-Ego concept of separateness. This process is an eternal circle which draws us into belonging!

UILE offers a different sort of home, where only Love is certain, yet peace fills the air like a summer day. Welcome back to the home you always longed for, where intentional freedom is found within. Home is where all is well, and you can drink from it today.

Summary

- Universal Intentional Love Energy is within you.
- You belong and are accepted within UILE without threat or coercion.
- Relationship is in all meaning, so embrace yourself, embrace change, solitary contemplation, and most of all, others.
- Thank you for reading this book, I hope it has raised your energy levels!

The Beginning.

About the Author

Phil "Philosofree" Cheney
B.Ec, Cert Bus. Stud, MACS, FIDA.

Phil is an Australian executive coach who lives with his wife Manu and her daughter in Toronto, Canada. Phil has two beautiful daughters and three grandchildren living in Australia.

He has travelled to over forty countries, and worked as a CEO, Director, IT analyst, soldier, policeman, consultant, marketer, producer, builder, musician and university lecturer.

During 2013 he wrote a poetry anthology called "Songs Above Notes". In 2015 he is writing the final book in the *Bion & Freya Trilogy*, mystery novels about life, love and meaning. His adventures have led to joint business ventures in exotic places which are included in his trilogy.

Phil's first book was a co-authored children's book called *Ernie and the Water Dwellers*, and he has also successfully created, written and produced two musicals, 450 poems, 250 songs, 5 paintings, over 20 Enterprise software modules, several houses and many short stories, some of which are on his blog. (www.diamondmine.me/blog)

A composer of many styles, Phil plays guitar and also enjoys writing, singing and playing music.

"I have used up all my nine cat's lives in many adventures, such as wrestling a seven foot long shark from the ocean with my bare hands!

Life is full of vibrancy and I love to play music and dance in celebration, which I do every week playing jazz, blues and covers at a restaurant in Toronto.

For me, meaning and connection are exemplified by family and friends, a Universal Intentional Love Energy which I write about in my non-fiction work, UILE.

I welcome the crossing of your path with mine, in fun or in the lessons of pain, both of which shape my life with creativity and understanding. Feel free to connect!"

Connect with Phil "Philosofree" Cheney

I really appreciate you reading this book!
Here are my social media coordinates:

Email me:
Philosofree@diamondmine.me
Friend me on Facebook:
http://facebook.com/PhilosofreeCheney
Follow me on Twitter:
http://twitter.com/_Philosofree
Connect on LinkedIn:
http://www.linkedin.com/in/Philosofree
Visit my websites:
http://www.advantace.com (Executive and Spiritual Coaching)
http://www.DiamondMine.me (Music and Art and blog)

Other books by this author

Fiction

The Bion & Freya Trilogy
Bion & Freya – Red Key – Asia & South America
Bion & Freya – Flight – North America & Europe
Bion & Freya – Scam – Africa & Australia (Due November 2015)

Poetry Series

Songs Above Notes – gratitude, humor and joy
Death of the Sun – renewal after suicide, grief and the loss of a child
(Available on request.)

Acknowledgements

I could not have written this book without those who have believed in me, most importantly my darling wife, Manuela "Manu" Cheney (www.smartieknows.com) and my friends who have spent time reading and editing drafts.

Namaste ("I see UILE shine in you")

Notes & References

1 UILE is an old Irish word meaning "All, whole, wholly, all things or entirely". If you long for belonging, free to accept life in abundance and joy, without guilt, then this book offers help.

2 Negative-Ego is defined in Chapter 4 "Our Internal Self". Ego has two aspects, positive and negative. Negative-Ego is the pessimistic and deprecatory, built up from shame experience in your early life.

3 Olyo is the ancestor language of the Celts.

4 Emerging research into dark matter and dark energy proposes that 96 percent of physical reality is literally obscure. It seems that the observable physical realm is floating on a vast ocean of energy called the zero-point energy field or the quantum vacuum field. Such research demonstrates how our understanding of the universe will continue to change and emerge. C.f. the later chapter UILE in Science, Art and Spirituality.

5 Marcus Chown explains that "73 per cent of the mass of the Universe is dark energy. Discovered only in 1998, this invisible stuff fills all of space and it has repulsive gravity."

6 Simple mathematics show that if $E=MC^2$ (Energy equals Mass times the speed of light squared) then if you divide both sides by C^2 the equation becomes $M=E/C^2$. This means that Mass is equivalent to a lot of energy.

7 Brookhaven National Lab, the European Organization for Nuclear Research (CERN) and Fermilab have all generated matter by firing photons of light into a heavy atomic nucleus. This is called *pair production.*

8 Einstein's work on relativity in the first part of the 20th century proved that matter also has a formulaic relationship ($E=MC^2$) with energy and the speed of light. It was that

research that led to the conversion of matter back into energy, which is what happens in a nuclear reactor or atomic bomb. In the early decades of the 21st century there has been increasing scientific research regarding the linked nature of energy (E) to matter. Accepted scientific belief is that without matter (M), time could not exist, because time is an essential element of speed, which is in the equation (C). Another way of understanding this is to realize that time is a function of Energy divided by Mass. If Mass is zero then the denominator is zero which means that time is undefined.

9 Since the 19th century, many physicists have worked on a single integrated theory for the fundamental forces or energies of nature. These are called unified field theories, where "field" in this context means the theoretical entities in space that carry forces or energies between objects. The first of these was James Clerk Maxwell, a Scotsman, who in 1865 demonstrated that both electric and magnetic fields travel through space as waves moving at the speed of light. Albert Einstein is the best known of the many physicists who postulated a unified field theory. Modern unified field theory is an attempt to explain the four different ways or interactions via which all energy is carried within space. These are Strong, Electromagnetic, Weak and Gravitational interactions, all of which have different characteristics.

10 http://www.youtube.com/watch?v=J3xLuZNKhlY quotes Prof Derek Leinweber.

11 This conclusion is consistent with Hubble's Law. The theory does not explain why the latent energy, which of course must always have existed according to the first law of thermodynamics, suddenly decided to be converted into various subatomic particles.

12 Prof. Bruce Lipton, *The Honeymoon Effect,* p. 17.

13 Teleonomy is a recent (1960s) scientific word which represents the quality of purposefulness and of goal

directedness of living organism structures and functions to serve an overall purpose. It appears to be a synonym to intrinsic teleology for scientists who object to considering extrinsic teleology.

14 African acacia trees have been found to increase tannin production in their leaves to make it less attractive for kudu antelope to eat them. Acacias also release ethylene into the air causing downwind acacias up to 50 yards away to increase their tannin defense within 10 minutes. The defense alert has been called an 'alarm system' (Hughes 1990).

15 Masaru Emoto (b 1943) is a Japanese energy scholar who believes that human consciousness has an effect on the molecular structure of water. Emoto's water crystal experiments consist of exposing water in glasses to different thought, and then freezing and examining the aesthetics of the resulting crystals with microscopic photography. The results show stunning regular differences depending on the exposure to thought, consistent with the claims that playing music to vegetables helps them grow bigger and stronger.

16 Alfred North Whitehead, OM FRS (1861–1947) was an English mathematician and philosopher.

17 Thomas Nagel, *Mind and Cosmos: Why the Materialist Neo-Darwinian Conception of Nature Is Almost Certainly False.*

18 M Scott Peck, *The Road Less Travelled*, p. 96.

19 Neil Turok, *The Universe Within*, p. 80.

20 The amount of information possible to be held within a single qubit is exponentially more than what is possible with a single bit of a conventional computer, because the qubit holds 2n probability states based on quantum theory. Quantum computing is still in its infancy, but it is not science fiction.

21 The challenge of **A**rtificial **I**ntelligence is to see if human intelligence can be simulated on a computer. Currently, for example, chess is played better by AI computers than most

humans, and may soon win against any human.

22 Professor Bruce Lipton, *The Honeymoon Effect* p. 21.

23 Robert Burney, *Codependence/The Dance of Wounded Souls*.

24 Matt 5:5 from the Message translation of the Bible.

25 The next chapter discusses space in more detail.

26 Detailed explanation in *Endless Light* by David Aaron.

27 Richard Rohr describes non-dualistic thinking as "our ability to read reality in a way that is not judgmental, in a way that is not exclusionary of the part that we don't understand. When you don't split everything up according to what you like and what you don't like, you let it be what it is in itself, and you let it speak to you."

28 I was raised a Christian, and therefore have this as my faith heritage, so I will recall examples of Jesus more than say Buddhist or Islamic texts or examples. You can find similar stories and emphases within your own heritage.

29 Matthew 7:12 "The Message".

30 John 15:5-8 Jesus also said, "I am the Vine, you are the branches. When you're joined with me and I with you, the relation intimate and organic, the harvest is sure to be abundant. Separated, you can't produce a thing.

31 An idiot was originally defined as a person who "lives outside the social expectations" from *idios*; one's own, private.

32 This includes the experiences which we may feel are suffering. Consider pain, which alerts our body so we can care for a wound. It can be called suffering or blessing.

33 The name could also be Superconscious, because it is in this realm that we are connected to UILE.

34 Johnson, Robert A., *Balancing Heaven and Earth: A Memoir of Visions, Dreams, and Realizations*.

35 I am aware that there are possibly 10 or 11 dimensions in math, but the fourth dimension is special.

36 St. Teresa of Avila (1515-1582) quoted in p. 287 *Love Poem*

from God, by Daniel Ladinsky.

37 The mindboggling aspects of mass in atoms is one of many things nicely explained in: Fred A Wolf; *Taking the Quantum Leap: The New Physics for Non-Scientists.*

38 From the ancient Judaic concepts described in *Endless Light*, by David Aaron, p. 18.

39 *A Second Treasury of Kahlil Gibran*, p. 33.

40 The song *The Musician's Prayer* describes this well, it is available on my website, www.diamondmine.me

41 Eagleman, David, *Incognito: The secret lives of the brain*

42 Johnson, Robert A., *Balancing Heaven and Earth: A Memoir of Visions, Dreams, and Realizations..*

43 The Shadow is a term used by Jung to describe subconscious initiation of negativity. Since 1935, there has been an emergence of *co-dependent, outer-dependent or external dependence* labels from the 12-step programs. These terms all reflect some of what Richard Rohr calls "stinking thinking" related to the inner child, which is damaged by emotional wounds from others and then acts out through us. "Stinking thinking" is ignorance of Love within yourself, because of external reliance on others for love and acceptance.

44 Eagleman, David *Incognito* p. 193.

45 I recognize that we may be deluding ourselves about the extent to which we actually make decisions. Each of us is one aspect of UILE that cannot be understood as an individual. Eagleman says, *"A slight change in the balance of brain chemistry can cause large changes in behavior."* 'Incognito' p.157. However, if we see that everything is part of a single incomprehensible whole, our decisions can be seen as part of that whole, without blame. *"It is not clear how much the conscious you – as opposed to the genetic and neural you – gets to do any deciding at all."* 'Incognito' p. 162.

46 This was a track from the album *Australian Dream* which was produced in 2003 for the Australian Refugee Association.

47 Joseph Campbell, T*he Hero With a Thousand Faces,* 1972, Princeton University Press.

48 The Greeks invented the word energy, too, but it meant activity or operation, not the general understanding of the word that we started using since 1807, namely; *a concept of potential or active force that can be transformed between different forms.*

49 My definition is "the study of the intention of love".

50 Johnson, Robert A., *Balancing Heaven and Earth: A Memoir of Visions, Dreams, and Realizations.*

51 Eagleman, David *Incognito*, p. 5.

52 The story of the Pharisee and the Tax collector can be found in Luke 18 9-14 – Jesus said, "This tax man, not the other, went home made right with God. If you walk around with your nose in the air, you're going to end up flat on your face, but if you're content to be simply yourself, you will become more than yourself."

53 All major religions have a history of persecution of those who opposed their dogma, irrespective of the loving lives the 'heretics' may have led.

54 Jews, Christians and Islamic religions are all founded in the stories of Abraham, from whom the tribes of Israel descended. Jesus was a Jew, and Mohammed incorporated the Old Testament into his faith.

55 Johnson, Robert A., *Balancing Heaven and Earth: A Memoir of Visions, Dreams, and Realizations.*

56 (Sophocles. Oedipus. Tyr. 154; Euripides. Hippolytus.1373.)

57 Robert A Johnson, *Inner Work,* Harper Collins ISBN 0-06-250437-1.

58 Johnson, Robert A., *Balancing Heaven and Earth: A Memoir of Visions, Dreams, and Realizations.*

59 Robert Burney, *Codependence/The Dance of Wounded Souls.*

60 *From http://www.6seconds.org/about/*

61 John MacMurray *Reason and Emotion*, p. 47.

62 Johnson, Robert A., *Balancing Heaven and Earth: A Memoir of Visions, Dreams, and Realizations*.

63 This story is fully described in *Balancing Heaven and Earth: A Memoir of Visions, Dreams, and Realizations* by Johnson, Robert A. and Jerry M. Ruhl (Jul 21, 2009)

64 This example is drawn from http://www.artandplay therapy.com

65 Gary Yontef and Lynne Jacobs, This is from a chapter of the popular textbook, *Current Psychotherapies*, by Corsini and Wedding.

66 Robert Burney, *Co-dependence : the dance of the wounded soul*, p. 125.

67 2 Tim 2:15 (the Message).

68 Robert A Johnson explains, "We owe to Jung the concept of the psychological archetypes – the characteristic patterns that pre-exist in the collective psyche of the human race, that repeat themselves eternally in the psyches of individual human beings and determine the basic ways that we perceive and function as psychological beings." "Stinking thinking" is a psychological archetype.

69 St. Theresa of Avila (1515-1582) quoted in p. 295, *Love Poems from God*, Daniel Ladinsky.

70 *No-one is Alone* is a beautiful song by Stephen Sondheim – you can watch it on YouTube sung by Bernadette Peters.

71 Probably the first recorded women's liberationist, Julian asked why should she be denied the right to her beliefs just because she is a woman? She also believed that "Our Savior is our true Mother in whom we are endlessly born and out of whom we shall never come."

72 Marianne Williamson, *Return to Love: Reflections on the Principles of "A Course in Miracles"*.

73 From John Lennon's anthem, *Imagine*..

74 M Scott Peck, *The Road Less Travelled*, p. 1.

75 Robert Burney, *Codependence: The Dance of Wounded Souls*, p.

112.

76 Richard Rohr, "Falling Upward" p 83

77 Jesus said, "No one lights a lamp, then hides it in a drawer. It's put on a lamp stand so those entering the room have light to see where they're going. Your being is a lamp, lighting up your whole body. If you live wide-eyed in wonder and belief, your body shines with light. If you live squinty-eyed in greed and distrust, your body is a dank cellar. Keep your eyes open, your lamp burning, so you don't get musty and murky. Keep your life as well-lighted as your best-lighted room." Luke 11:33 – The Message.

78 Kahlil Gibran *Wisdom of Gibran*, p. 94.

79 The Christian statement of faith the Nicene Creed (current Ecumenical version) states, "We look for the resurrection of the dead, and the life of the world to come."

80 The Jewish religion believes in afterlife, but does not have strict dogma. Based on the Book of Revelation in the Bible, Christian belief holds that all true believers will spend eternity with God. Islamists believe in an afterlife that is similar to the Christian view.

81 If you haven't read Marianne Williamson's book *Return to Love* then I recommend you grab a copy!

82 As quoted in Daniel Ladinsky, *Love Poems from God*, p. 277.

83 Rachel Remen, *Kitchen Table Wisdom*.

84 http://www.stevebiddulph.com/

85 Story modified from Robert Burney's book on Co-dependence, p. 124.

86 John Tickell, *Laughter, Sex, Vegetables & Fish: 10 Secrets of Long Living People*.

87 Prof John MacMurray, *Reason and Emotion* p. 180.

88 P. 168-9, *Reason and Emotion* and following two quotes.

89 Prof John MacMurray, *Reason and Emotion*.

90 Paul Simon, lyrics from his song *Kodachrome* on his *Rhymin Simon* album.

91 A 44-year-old man's brain showed that a huge fluid-filled chamber called a ventricle took up most of the room in his skull, leaving little more than a thin sheet of actual brain tissue, yet he functions normally (2007). The Lancet (vol 370, p. 262). One of the latest theories is that memory is stored in the water within our body.

92 Joseph M Marshall III, *Returning to the Lakota Way*, p. 195.

93 Richard Rohr, *Breathing Under Water: Spirituality and the Twelve Steps*, pp. 11-13.

94 Rob Bell, from the lecture *What We Talk About When We Talk About God*, March 14, 2013 at Vanderbilt University.

CHRISTIAN
ALTERNATIVE

Throughout the two thousand years of Christian tradition there have been, and still are, groups and individuals that exist in the margins and upon the edge of faith. But in Christianity's contrapuntal history it has often been these outcasts and pioneers that have forged contemporary orthodoxy out of former radicalism as belief evolves to engage with and encompass the ever-changing social and scientific realities. Real faith lies not in the comfortable certainties of the Orthodox, but somewhere in a half-glimpsed hinterland on the dirt track to Emmaus, where the Death of God meets the Resurrection, where the supernatural Christ meets the historical Jesus, and where the revolution liberates both the oppressed and the oppressors.

Welcome to Christian Alternative... a space at the edge where the light shines through.